No Strings Attached

No Strings Attached

Breaking Free of
Political Manipulations
in the Mediascape.

Dr. Chris Homan and Thomas Dudek

Charleston, SC
www.PalmettoPublishing.com

No Strings Attached

Copyright © 2021 by Dr. Chris Homan
and Thomas Dudek

All rights reserved

No portion of this book may be reproduced,
stored in a retrieval system, or transmitted in any form
by any means–electronic, mechanical, photocopy,
recording, or other–except for brief quotations
in printed reviews, without prior permission
of the author.

First Edition

Hardcover ISBN: 978-1-63837-191-5
Paperback ISBN: 978-1-63837-192-2
eBook ISBN: 978-1-63837-190-8

From Chris: To my Mom and Dad,
who always made it clear how important
it was for me to develop a sense of political literacy.

From Thomas: To my beloved Benita,
whom I've grown with politically,
and who makes me a better consumer.

Those who are too smart to engage in politics are punished by being governed by those who are dumber.

—Plato

CONTENTS

Prologue xi

I.	Rope-a-Dope	1
II.	Dance to the Beat of your Own Drum	10
III.	Making Our Way through the Labyrinth	17
IV.	Reading the Fine Print	33
V.	That's Entertainment!	53
VI.	We Get by with a Little Help from Our Friends	62
VII.	Make a Good Argument	76
VIII.	Politics and Piracy	87
IX.	Knowing is Half the Battle	96
X.	Making Voices Heard through the Art of Storytelling	111

Relevant Reading and All-Round Useful Information 123

PROLOGUE

Be first the master of yourself.

—Balthasar Gracian,
The Art of Worldly Wisdom

Politics directly and profoundly affect all our lives. It is nothing less than the process of influencing social behavior. It's how a citizenry determines how to work together, behave, and establish standards for civilization. Everything is political, and it always has been. Political thoughts are what dictate what you can do and the words you say, and how you exercise these affects the options you cultivate throughout your life. The political is personal, and the personal is political. Ideally, everyone who affects the political process is educated and informed about the issues and, publicly or privately, works toward standards that are helpful to everyone else.

Unfortunately this does not usually happen.

Wars are declared when philosophies clash, trade sanctions are enacted to flex economic might over weaker players, and special interest groups manipulate and deceive people into promoting their agenda. People all too often support causes and ideas without a full understanding of the facts because they are either misinformed, distracted, or have become victims of groupthink.

See George Orwell's *1984* for more information about groupthink.

Political control of the masses is a cunningly orchestrated process, and we all succumb to its pressure without realizing it. Just as every successful market and store has features that lure us in, every politician, media outlet, and talking head makes their agenda so attractive to us, we accept it into our minds and hearts without being aware we are being manipulated against our better nature.

From our experience people are interested in politics but don't always feel as if they possess the understanding to speak cogently about it due to perceived ignorance. Political literacy reflects a capacity for citizens to critically reflect upon political institutions and processes, even their own, and determine for themselves the values of such institutions and processes. By empowering all citizens to express political opinions formed after honest and brave introspection, society might raise the political literacy of its citizens. Many of us feel, for some reason, that once we hit eighteen years of age, we achieve enlightenment overnight and then must participate on some level as well-meaning citizens.

Perhaps we get this feeling because, in certain societies, people suddenly get voting power overnight. When you're eighteen, you can vote. In some countries this is when you are allowed to drive a car; in most countries this is when people can buy alcohol and cigarettes legally. This is an odd position to maintain since most schools don't take the time to help us vocalize what kind of a society we wish to live in. Schools, typically, don't teach students enough about what it means to be a citizen and how students can make their voices heard. Most citizens are indoctrinated without honest cultural examination.

A parent's ability to afford medical care for their sick relative comes down to politics because the system has been shaped by the actions, or inactions, of people in power. How a society's police force treats the citizenry, how prison systems accommodate those that have been deemed to be criminals, and how systems of justice operate are all guided by people's political philosophies. Whether or not people are able to marry the person they love or are forced to marry someone they don't is political. People fearing they will be deported from their homes comes down to surrounding politics. A person's impressions about humanity's effects on the environment correspond to their politics. Declaring peace, going to war, hanging a flag, and singing anthems are political philosophies.

Most people don't talk much about politics. Even you probably prefer to wait to expose your political leanings only when you're around a trusted few, in safe spaces, accompanied only by those who are secure enough in their philosophies to invite dissenting opinions. Interesting ideas about how to improve government, remedy socioeconomical failings, or educate the culture, no matter how innocent, relevant, or constructive, are largely consigned to the darkest halls of silence if they are of a political nature.

And these thoughts *are* of a political nature.

The lack of political literacy around the world partly corresponds with apathy among citizens, especially young citizens. This happens because political topics are almost always discussed in such boring and complex terms, most intelligent and hopeful people feel like they can't understand any of it, and so they get frustrated and tune out, instead choosing to focus on shinier facets of living. This voluntary abstinence pleases those political players who wish to discourage people from participating in any meaningful decision-making process so they can better control an uninformed populace.

People can feel that campaign promises are meaningless because there is no accountability. Often people resign from participation in politics because whomever they vote for does not get elected anyways or if they do, they follow the same path, processes, and actions all previous leaders have taken. People may feel it's pointless to vote since the outcome doesn't matter. There are citizens who think that participating in the system grants legitimacy to the idea that it's acceptable for the state to impose their will on the people by threat of force, and for that reason, some believe it is immoral to participate. Some feel that any political gesture reinforces the idea that people can't live together without control, that those in power know what's best, often by the threat of violence against peaceful people. Many claim that political action is futile because only rich people, not ordinary people, win.

The likelihood that people will be equipped to make an informed choice is, in our opinion, not great if the only information a person has is from news channels, politicians, and political parties without verifying claims through unbiased and more authentic sources. Some think that they do more for their community by not participating in its politics rather than being part of or supporting a pretentious system. Some societies make it difficult for citizens to participate by actively making the participation process cumbersome. Those with an agenda know that easier processes could mean more participation of the population. Many people experience impostor syndrome, so they don't participate. They believe they don't understand enough about the government, the election process, or controversial policies. Rather than feeling empowered by having a vote, the opposite happens, and people feel powerless or even helpless.

Showing loyalty to communal values continues to be a significant part of social bonding. People are highly social and observe others' behaviors and, in many cases, follow their lead. This can go either way, depending on what most others do or don't do. For example, if the social group doesn't regard politics as very important, a person may not bother to participate either.

Then there are those who just aren't interested. Most people consume information through social media echo chambers rather than reliable sources, which can leave people feeling disillusioned and cynical toward politics. It's more than just a shame that people aren't better motivated to participate in political processes. As Edmund

Burke said, "The only thing necessary for the triumph of evil is for good men to do nothing."

Each of us are either buying something or selling something. When you apply for a job, you are convincing someone that you are a worthwhile attribute that they should desire. When siblings fight over what the family should eat for dinner, they are each making a case for their own tastes and preferences. Our values, desires, passions, opinions, and efforts are tied to political expression. How we successfully express our politics depends on what we know or more accurately, what we think we know. It can sometimes be difficult to articulate to others our political values, but that doesn't make us any less committed to our passions.

Political literacy means knowing a thing or two about the political information that comes into your life, and honing our sense of political literacy helps us to keep from feeling like imposters in our own lives. Politically literate people know more than simply the names and political parties of presidential candidates who are campaigning for the next election. Such individuals make themselves aware of as much of the political process and political affairs as they can to fulfill their roles as responsible citizens. Politically literate people are usually aware of the issues the campaigning individuals espouse, and they have a desire to maintain the skills that allow them to navigate political themes—the same way a parent shops only at the stores that offer good deals on groceries and doesn't get fooled into buying things they regret. Although we are not politicians or political insiders, we feel like we can suggest ways in which someone can become a more politically literate person. It is our position that just because something is uncertain or not what it claims to be, it shouldn't mean that we disengage ourselves from spheres of influence that benefit from our participation.

Becoming more politically literate means improving three individual aspects we all have: cognitive awareness, attitude, and behavior. Ensuring that we have sufficient and accurate information about political topics and situations allows each of us to form a dependable philosophy to guide our actions, thoughts, and opinions. To be informed, most of us are flooded by an unending stream of political information and news. There is so much input from everywhere, all the time, it overwhelms the senses. Most people do not make the time to verify or cross-check what they are told, so their conversations and actions are guided by incorrect data. Everyone in the world is entitled to speak their mind, not only the self-declared experts or the privileged minority, but it seems most of us are led to believe that it is otherwise. This makes for a politically illiterate population that can be controlled and manipulated, leaving its societies vulnerable to making decisions that are fueled by misinformation and ignorance.

All over the world, intelligent and hopeful creatures like us are made to feel like we must avoid certain topics, to keep silent as misinformation swirls around us at dinner tables, on trains, in workplaces, and even in our beds. More and more we are avoiding topics that we think might step on people's toes, letting ourselves become intimidated by political issues. We feel like we are outnumbered by a misinformed opposition, or maybe we are too distracted by an overworked life to care.

When people come together to grab a bite to eat, celebrate a birthday, attend service, or catch up together after several years apart, political topics can be a delicate affair. It is all but universally accepted that politics are not to be brought up, and anything that can be seen as political must be consigned to forbidden territory lest the sky catch on fire from the heat of inconsolable differences in opinions. People would rather discuss uncontroversial topics, even though everyone present is a functioning member of society with fully formed ideas, even if they have genuine questions about the issues covered by the media, the state of the economy, the actions of world leaders, or the state of military activity. Nobody wants to be the person who causes the awkward silence. Verboten topics include family gossip, money, and politics. So, conversations mill around sports, television, the weather, and shopping.

It is our shared opinion that people don't participate in the political process enough and that we as a society are made to consistently give rise to leaders who work against our interests. We argue that there is a growing and pressing need for a more politically literate society.

Suppose we lived in a world where political conversations did not need to be unpleasant, aggressive, or a source of resentment? What if human beings had more in common than they thought, and discussing the issues that really matter in the world didn't threaten to turn sibling against sibling? What if people felt like they were qualified to discuss current events and political decisions with each other, without fear of being ostracized?

What a wonderful environment of idea sharing and problem solving. What a wonderful place this would be, where people from different cultures and of various philosophies would listen to each other without being made to feel like they had to abandon their most cherished values. Such a populace would have to be willing to learn beyond what they thought they already knew and work to overcome their egos, even if it meant occasionally being humble and accepting new ideas. But we live in this one, where political topics are vulgar and unsafe.

Fine. Let's not talk about politics.

People love talking about where they got their fancy new shoes, Grandpa's brand-new fishing rod, their first car, or the house big enough for the family to host guests. All our lives we are inducted into conversations about how we acquired the things we have brought into our lives and homes. These are conversations that are safe and full of necessary information, no matter what the occasion is, what country the conversation is taking place in, or what the personal philosophies are of the conversationalists.

Shopping can be fun, but even visiting a simple Middle Eastern market may make shoppers feel overwhelmed if they aren't aware of what merchants and the shopping environment do to affect their decision-making. Experienced vendors all over the world have a good eye for what shoppers are like. When you enter their shop or browse their stall, skilled merchants can tell immediately from your body language whether you are street-smart or not. If you are relatively comfortable and experienced with the local traditions, nobody can take advantage of your naiveté and you can negotiate a transaction for the merchandise that you desire. Some sellers might think that you already spent some time at this place and know the ropes. If you come to a transaction without having prepared yourself by doing research or observing the local customs, you will likely pay too much for something or make a purchase that you will later become unhappy with.

What relative doesn't want to hear about the latest bargain? What bedouin isn't curious about where to get the best deal on a flock of sheep or herd of camels? What parent doesn't want to know which grocery stores sell the freshest produce for the lowest price? What kid isn't interested in getting as much candy as they can for their pocket money? Even people with money to waste want to know where and how to spend their money advantageously.

What if we started looking at the news and politics the same way we looked at shopping?

I
Rope-a-Dope

Until you realize how easily it is for your mind to be manipulated, you remain the puppet of someone else's game.

—Evita Ochel

Let's talk about dopamine (bear with us, it will become relevant soon). Dopamine is a chemical in our brains that allows us to feel pleasure. It's a feel-good neurotransmitter that is released when we eat food, exercise, have sex, or do other pleasurable things contributing to the mental feelings of pleasure and satisfaction. Dopamine improves our mood, powers our motivation, and focuses our attention when we need it to raise our performance levels. This chemical does more than reward us when we behave a certain way; it is a big part of how we think and plan. It helps us strive to make great efforts and find things interesting that don't seem worth the effort to others. While we may not know everything about dopamine, we do know that it is a significant ingredient in our actions and decisions.

With some awareness of our environments and ourselves, we can avoid having our dopamine levels manipulated, which can lead us to do what we might not do in our right minds—like when we are vulnerable, in over our heads, in enemy territory, being subjugated by tools and tactics that mostly operate below our radar.

Just like in a supermarket.

What we suggest here is that *you're* not like everyone else. *You're* a thinking human being! You're not some witless sheep to be led around! You'd never walk out of the store with more than you intended to buy, right?

Except that one time. Well, a few times.

Come on, it's human nature to make decisions on the fly!

Our point is that it's just a few extra items that you probably wanted anyway, you just didn't know were available, you were going to get someday anyway. No big deal.

But it is a big deal.

The moment you walk into a grocery store, your dopamine levels are being targeted and activated. No matter if you spend five minutes in a 7-Eleven or three hours in EverythingMart, the dopamine in your brain is increased by subtle actors that go mostly unnoticed by your senses. The environment you have entered is content rich and professionally designed to captivate the attention of any shopper, even the attention of those who only want to make a quick purchase. But not just our attention is being targeted. Perhaps even more importantly, marketers target our *in*attention. They want you—all of us—not to be attentive, to make impulsive decisions.

Supermarket builders and store architects have known for decades that a person can go from a dedicated shopper to an indecisive shopper to an emotional shopper and then to a brand-driven shopper if they are in a certain mindset. Manipulating a person's dopamine level helps to change a person from "I'm only going to the store for some gravy" to "I've got the best deal ever on a dozen pineapples! What are we going to do with all these pineapples now?"

Stores bombard all your senses the moment you walk through the door. The manipulation begins with the tiniest attention to detail, a detail so small you may not be able to sniff it out or be aware that sniffing it out is exactly what you are doing. Ever noticed baked goods, fresh produce, the delicatessen, and even the flowers are usually located right by the front of the store? Right away you'll smell the cookies, breathe in the flowers, and more than likely, you're thinking about chasing that dopamine high. As you walk through the area that smells like a nutritious, life-giving garden, you might be encouraged on some level to linger a little longer around the vibrant fruits and veggies on display, whose colors almost leap into your field of vision.

As you head to get that gravy, you can't help but notice that there are some warm blueberry muffins on sale, and wouldn't they go so well with some of that nearby Amish churned butter that's featured in that nearby display! Sure, you just ate a big lunch an hour ago, but man, don't you just want some of those warm blueberry muffins? This is all a ploy to make you feel hungry. When you're hungry, you buy more. It's just about impossible to walk through any major store in the world without smelling a fresh batch of baguettes or pizza that you can't resist. It's fairly simple, and devilishly logical.

Being hungry affects your decision-making ability. Studies showed that hunger affects people's buying decisions, including those around nonfood items. These studies showed that shoppers are more likely to buy unnecessary items impulsively the hungrier they are. USC Professor Norbert Schwarz tells us that "the desire to get food may more generally plant the idea of 'getting stuff' in your mind, which increases the likelihood that you'll also be attracted to products that won't satisfy your physical hunger…the internal message 'I want food' becomes simply 'I want.'"

Most shoppers that walk into any given supermarket are unaware they're being handled by an elegantly intricate and complex smell warfare designed to get unsuspecting human beings hungry and susceptible to flexible shopping decisions. Colorful products and sweet-smelling baked goods aren't the only ways grocery stores try to activate your salivary glands. Popular chains all provide single-serving samples for consumers to try. After tasting that new flavor of Coca-Cola, that new low-fat ice cream, that new chocolate-covered cheesecake, there's a good chance that you'll want to buy some of those products for your family, now that more senses are being played with than just your vision.

Just like that you're walking out with your gravy. Plus four other items you didn't plan on purchasing. It won't be until after some time, after your dopamine levels have settled back to normal, that you wonder what was so great about all these extra purchases and if it was worth it to spend so much. You may even suddenly begin to question your own reasoning that seemed so logical during the shopping exercise. "Will my friends even like this new pomegranate flavored tea? What am I going to do with all these tomatoes? Do my kids even like pineapple?" Such thoughts may lead to buyer's remorse, panic, and regret.

* * *

Although it means being mindful of external stimulations that are trying to play with dopamine levels, it is entirely possible to maintain self-control. We humans might be functions of our environments, but we are not brainless zombies. The same goes for when we watch television. Although our brains are in a more vulnerable, more accessible place whenever we're consuming hours of televised news and entertainment, we can take steps to guard against outside forces playing with our decision-making processes.

Consider the possibility that watching movies, television series, and the news is a passive habit that more and more of the world is succumbing to. After a certain amount of time, we lose track of how long we've been staring at the monitor or screen because our dopamine levels have risen, and it begins to feel good.

Real good. *Addictive*, even.

But we need to stay informed about what goes on in the world, right? Watching the news is easier than reading about it and since we can multitask, is a more efficient use of time. We can make a pot of coffee, feed the dog, and knit a pair of socks as official channels let us know what politicians are up to and what disasters to avoid. If sources inform us about current events and tell us what is relevant to our lives, what is there to worry about?

Just like walking into the dopamine-inducing superstore, watching lots of television day after day taps into the human brain subliminally and plays with our dopamine. This has the guaranteed result of making us a receptive audience with less mindfulness than we might suspect. Without being aware of what is happening to our brain chemicals, we are completely ignorant to the impulses we might feel when presented with perceived dangers and local threats.

Good thing the news never shows us that kind of content, right? Otherwise we might be led to form longstanding and deeply held opinions about people, systems, and places that we have very little experience or interaction with. Opinions that are subtly and repetitively fed to us in such a way that makes us think that we formed said opinions on our own, without manipulation or outside interference. But that couldn't possibly be happening all around the world on a constant basis, right? The good news (pun intended) is that becoming mindful consumers of the news frees us to be more guarded, defensive even, when we are confronted with the bubble presented by the headlines, opinion pieces, and the authoritative voices of the media.

You may be shocked by the thought of the news actively manipulating your decision-making center, but that is exactly what happens on a massive level. It is made even more possible by the nearly drugged state the mind enters when being bombarded by hours of television, which we sometimes subject ourselves to when we follow a particularly harrowing story, learn about a change in the economy, or perceive suspicious threats to our way of life. Good news is rarely emphasized in the news cycle, but that isn't the fault of the news stations—they are just giving us the headlines that are going to keep our attention. After a while immersing ourselves in disasters and the pain of others, how can we look away or stop following the stories if we are certain that bad guys are on their way to world domination?

We learn to feel good by scanning for information that is relevant to our survival. The more information-processing capacity we expend on digesting the news, the less there is to process other, more survival-relevant information. Science suggests that the brain only has limited resources and capacity, and every new piece of information, every daily decision (out of the tens of thousands we make every day) depletes these resources and occupies our minds. When engaged in an activity that produces dopamine, the body is internally rewarded with a pleasurable feeling that we might not even notice and that is sure to encourage continued engagement in said activity. Continued television watching, even in the name of following current events, reinforces the brain with signals that communicate to the body that said activity is good, to keep doing it. The brain is going to keep on producing dopamine, fueling a drug-like high that fosters an addiction to televised news to attempt to satisfy our cravings for more and more dopamine.

Watching the news is so tempting because the information that is presented is so easily available, we are conditioned to think that it is the truth, and we are assured that this information is what we need to be responsible citizens and perhaps to survive. Our minds are further led to construct dopamine pathways so we feel good when we learn how some story turns out and when we form a determined opinion about a politician or social system. Whether or not watching the news meets our social needs, we are encouraged to follow the news to feel good. Watching the news feeds into our quest for survival by gathering information that we perceive to be relevant, even if the information we get doesn't actually meet that need.

The trouble with spending too much time upping our dopamine on news is that our valuable time and attention can easily become squandered on generalized threats that we can't act against or be expected to do much about. Just like in a grocery store, we can quickly get caught up in the smells of the warm blueberry muffins and be distracted from our mission to buy only gravy, even though there is more than enough food at home. By keeping mindful as we enter the store, we can stick to the task and get what we need, only what we need, without wasting money, attention, or time.

Similarly, we can remain mindful as we gather information from the news. Rather than avoiding the news altogether, it might be possible to manage our own dopamine stimulation by choosing how we access the media and manage how the media accesses us. Rather than submit to the obscene wealth of prepared information of televised outlets and news generators, we can glance at the news in manageable chunks, then chase the information we want to learn more about on our own, through trusted online sources and among the real people in our lives. Yet even in doing this, we need to be aware that news providers know well how to capture our attention and make us seek more information. Learning about the events that are covered in the news on our own terms can help us to hone the abilities that allow us to navigate obstacles, like dopamine traps and counterintuitive decision-making. What we constantly need to do, however, is become aware of the traps the news providers and marketers set for us. Like warm blueberry muffins, watching too much televised news occupies our minds by temporarily satisfying some of our desires. Only when we begin to understand the susceptibility of our happy mind chemicals can we act in ways that waste less time, allow us to keep in our right minds, and allow us to feel just as good.

II
Dance to the Beat of your Own Drum

*My soul, I've found, has puppet strings to make us droop
or give us wings. And music is the puppeteer
that turns my ear to hear.*

—Richelle E. Goodrich, *Slaying Dragons*

We love music. Nothing stimulates the mind quite like music. It can lift our mood, get us energized, or make us feel calm and relaxed. Music allows us to feel just about all the emotions that we can possibly experience throughout our lives. It's almost impossible to imagine stores, shops, and supermarkets without music; many of us cannot do without it while traveling. Here, music does not really relax but rather makes it easy to deal with stress. Music arouses emotions, and what people feel when listening to a piece of music and how they act on those feelings can be, and often is, influenced by others. Even if it all happens on an unconscious level, we are manipulated every time we hear music.

Music deeply affects people's mood, and there are so many ways to use its influence. That background music that your ears barely register whenever you're in a store isn't the courteous touch that you might think it is. It's there to lull you into a more susceptible state as research tells us that certain types of music affect our behavior. A study by the American Marketing Association found that music that was upbeat generated more sales than slower music did. The music that stores play affects the rate at which people roam the aisles and has a direct effect on the amount of money people spend.

Stores that play music see increased sales, but only with certain types of music. Cheerful music subliminally persuades us to buy more than we would otherwise because our moods and attitudes are gently lifted without us being aware. When that music is then played at a slow tempo, it can make us buy more by making us linger for longer in the aisles, opening up a greater opportunity for us to admire the wondrous produce around us, making it more likely for us to buy them.

Studies show that at around twenty-three minutes, shoppers make choices with the emotional part of their brain instead of the logical. Scientists make a fairly clear distinction between the emotional brain (called system 1 thinking)—which is automatic and makes decisions based on experiences and intuition—and the rational brain (called system 2 thinking)—which we use for deliberate, effortful decisions that require our consciousness. But the problem with our system 2 "rational" brain is that it has limited resources and capacity. After forty minutes (the average time of a weekly shopping trip), the brain stops making rational thoughts altogether. This illustrates with alarming certainty that the longer people are in a grocery store, the more impulse buys and unnecessary purchases are made.

Store music need not be seen simply as a negative. As long as we keep it in mind that the music is there and don't let the dulcet tones sway us into a commercialized stupor, we and most other customers are likely to feel like we had a positive experience shopping. Even if we spent most of our time in the store looking for items that don't exist (like delicious vegetarian bacon or carb-free pizza), watching the guy ahead of us in the ten-items-or-less checkout line pretend that he doesn't see the sign as he unloads his overflowing shopping cart, or waiting to speak to a customer service associate (to report violations witnessed in the ten-items-or-less checkout line).

Perhaps we shouldn't be so abrasive toward shop and store designers. Perhaps all these food center architects and supermarket providers are just being thoughtful benefactors who know only that we customers respond positively when they play a certain type of music at a certain tempo and volume. Perhaps these kind souls are merely making us feel our most comfortable, the way we would welcome a guest to a comfortable stay in our home. Music tends to cause people to think about their role in society and focus on their own self-expression, even as they're comparing tomatoes. One study found that shoppers' preference for French or German wine shifted in a way that corresponded according to which country's traditional music was playing from a nearby set of speakers.

Emotional music makes us more likely to feel happiness, sadness, excitement, and music with a cognitive function can lead us to feel removed from our world—or feel engaged. Intensity of the melodies and too much emotional arousal can be a bad thing, as studies on the volume of in-store music on shoppers' behavior have detailed. Arousal-focused music excites our senses and invites us to action. Whenever we humans are enjoying ourselves by listening to music we like, it doesn't matter what the setting is. Even if we're fighting crowds of people for that too-good-to-believe deal, the experience becomes more pleasant, leading us to value that time more than we might have if no music was played at all.

If you have personally experienced what shopping is like without music, then you might know just how different an experience shopping can be. Although if you happen to be shopping in stores during electrical blackouts in various locations such as Saudi Arabia, India, or the Philippines, where stores don't necessarily have a sound system, the shopping experience is more sober on a subliminal, almost imperceptible level, even if the selection and the environment is pleasant enough to be in.

To achieve more effective sales rates, shop managers know that the music in the background must be low enough to allow shoppers to think about their purchases but loud enough for us to detect. Using tempo, volume, genre, and combining music selections with certain sensory influences, like smart scent marketing, affects the spending habits of many customers who walk through supermarket doors.

* * *

At this point we can agree that music is powerful when we are barely aware of it. It stands to reason, then, that music might have an even more profound effect on us when we are conscious of it. When we listen to music that is composed with the distinct, singular purpose of communicating something, listeners are certain to receive that message loud and clear. Messages carried by music, especially when there are no words, can be fascinating. Musical structures are often arranged in multiple layers, and without any mental effort on our part as listeners, our emotions are affected. When music goes silent, we are usually aware of the change in mood.

Music plays an important, and sometimes overlooked, function in our culture. Music touches us emotionally. It touches our memories and our dreams. Military bands still perform a vital function for our armed servicemen and servicewomen and for society. During World War II, military music was used to galvanize troops to drive into battle with drums, flutes, and trumpets. Heroic fanfare welcomed troops back to their homeland and let everyone know when it had been a victorious campaign. The music that was played during and after military efforts went a long way toward boosting troop morale, helping society to go along with the war effort, and integrating troops back into their homelives, even when they were suffering internally from their undisclosed traumas, long before therapists, counselors, or legalized marijuana.

There is an entire industry dedicated to the sole purpose of background music that employs sensory marketing, which yearns to determine what we hear as we go about our everyday business in certain places. Store builders and shop designers believe psychologists who think that music can have two kinds of effects on listeners. The first effect is physical. Numerous studies suggest that we tend to subconsciously match what we are doing to what we hear. The second is music's ability to trigger certain perspectives according to the context and the environment we are in. For example, most of us associate classical music with quality. People respond to music differently depending on the setting in which they are exposed to it.

It isn't just supermarket designers who are interested in the relationship between music and listener behavior. Media channels are putting to excellent use the reliable effects music has when played in certain contexts. Television news has been using music to manipulate listener emotions subtly. News broadcasts have created a well-known patchwork of "opens," "rejoins," "bumpers," and "closes" to guide television audiences through the telecast. The music is a major part of what keeps viewers tuned to news channels and glued to the screen because the music makes viewers feel that the next news segment can't be ignored, no matter who is presenting or what the headlines are. The authenticity of the channel, station, or news team is unquestionable because the music we watch the news to establishes a branding identity that is no-nonsense and the people we are watching speak out of our televisions are to be trusted.

Most importantly the important-sounding music makes us feel that we are irresponsible citizens if we disengage from the stream of information. Good citizenry and human curiosity make us interested in the news; the music makes us digest the news broadcasts in enormous servings. Aaron Copland's *Fanfare for the Common Man* inspired broadcast music with power and purity that elevated watching the news into an important event rather than a pastime. Using music, the news started to be presented in a far more manipulative way than ever before. This went a long way toward influencing how viewers interpreted current events. Music is still used to manipulate emotionally and connect more intimately than most news reports ever could on their own.

Some of us might be uncomfortable with the thought of having our minds and hearts played with by stores and news broadcasts through music. It seems to us that the answer to keeping our wits about us as we gather our groceries and stay informed about world events is to be aware of the conditions we immerse ourselves in. By being aware of the music of a place or a televised report, we can acknowledge the sounds consciously (with our system 2 brain) rather than only by our emotions. This subtle step up in our attentive process might help us to keep hold of our decision-making processes rather than succumb to buying unnecessary blueberry muffins or being glued to a news channel and being spoon-fed opinions that we might not otherwise have had about what is going on in the world. Other steps we can take in these matters are listening to our own personal music, audiobooks, podcasts, etcetera as we shop or watching the news with the volume off. Who knows, maybe these simple yet powerful actions might have positive effects on our everyday habits, prolonged routines, and our lives.

III
Making Our Way through the Labyrinth

*We are, as a species, addicted to story.
Even when the body goes to sleep,
the mind stays up all night, telling itself stories.*

—Jonathan Gottschall, *The Storytelling Animal*

Who we are, specifically, what kind of shopper we are before we walk into a shop, matters greatly when it comes to our mission once inside. Without a mission, without direction to guide us, we allow ourselves to be susceptible to the manipulations inside. Every shop and supermarket can be a minefield—for some scientists and marketers, we may even say a min*d*field—if you don't have your presence of mind or aren't mindful of why you're there. Knowing who you are and what you want can be empowering, giving you the ability to be a more intelligent shopper before entering a store. We think that self-awareness is a necessary basis for resisting the possibility of being lulled into unintended purchases, which makes going grocery shopping a happier and more fulfilling experience.

Self-awareness has been a subject of deep philosophical thought. One of Socrates' most profound maxims tell us how important is to "know thyself." Who are we to think that self-awareness is anything but a cornerstone of identity and intelligence, as well as our ability to know our preferences, resources, and intuitions? Surely we can all agree that only when we are self-aware are we free to act on the knowledge we have acquired from the world around us and apply it as agents of free will. People who are self-aware are more likely to act deliberately, mindfully, and consciously rather than merely react to their environments. Self-aware shoppers spend their time and money better and make more informed choices from the selections offered. Knowing what type of person you are and what your decision-making process is like allows you to break from the mild stupor that you are tempted to enter while shopping. If you are able to keep your head, you are more likely to stop and think about why you want to buy something rather than end up with an expensive pile of goods that you never intended to purchase.

If you are a frugal shopper or discount hunter, do your homework about in-store specials before browsing the store. If you are going to the store for a list of only things that you need, focus on finding only the items you want for that trip. Prepare that shopping list before you make your way to the store, and always keep it handy, and try not to deviate from it. If all you need from a shop to make a purchase is the best price, be sure that is what you are getting, and do so in a timely fashion. If you're a brand name shopper, consider the possibility that you might leave the store empty-handed if the selection doesn't offer exactly what you demand. If you have a fixed budget, do like your parents and grandparents and great-grandparents—make a shopping list, compare prices, and make a determined effort to learn which stores have the lowest prices. If you think of yourself as a practical shopper, don't let yourself fall for pretty packaging, fancy advertising, or subliminal messages. If you are a social shopper, you might care about what your friends and peers are purchasing. In this case ask their opinions before making your purchase. Perhaps *they* aren't even satisfied with their purchase, with the product, or about why they made the purchase decision in the first place.

Even with all the ways to acquire information, word of mouth still ranks highly in personal view. Perhaps you love putting yourself in the hands of marketers and don't mind making a trip to the supermarket with hardly any idea of what you actually want or need. Maybe you like the experience of shopping itself, whether it's online or in a brick-and-mortar store. It could very well be that shopping is one of your favorite hobbies and the commercial exchange is what delights you whenever you have time to spend on yourself. Then again, you may be an indecisive shopper who isn't sure what you are looking for and may not be comfortable going with the first thing you see.

If you take nothing else from this book but this, you'll be one step closer to making more economical decisions and being freed from marketers' manipulations: always take your time and consider how a product you're thinking of buying will affect your life. Sure, organic spinach claims to be healthier, but is it really? Is it worth paying twice as much for it if you have less money to get other groceries? Do you really need it, or is your purchase consideration only a sudden feeling of need? Do you know where this feeling of need came from? Do you miss this item/product when you're at home?

Now that you have taken the time to realize who you are and, by extension, your purpose, before you enter the store, you are prepared to explore the labyrinth that awaits. The next challenge is to be aware that it has been uniquely and thoroughly constructed to distract you from your mission, entertain you, sell you more than you desire, take more of your money than you want, and direct your mind, heart, and body toward what's best for the store—it all more often than not works *against* you, not *for* you. For example, have you ever noticed that there are hardly ever any windows in grocery stores? When was the last time you saw a clock on a supermarket wall? Stores, malls, and supermarkets are deliberately designed to make shoppers, no matter what kind, lose track of their time. Unless you have plenty of time and money and are okay with being taken for a ride on someone else's terms, this is a well-crafted manipulation. Being in a timeless space encourages most people to take longer to do their shopping and consequently spend more money. The size of the shopping venue matters as well. When a venue is crowded, shoppers spend less time there, make fewer purchases, and feel less comfortable than they do at a place that is less crowded. Stores have found a solution to the crowded problem by getting bigger and bigger. Therefore, each location feels less crowded, and every shopper is encouraged to stay longer.

Once you are inside, it may go unnoticed to the untrained or distracted eye that all the aisles, displays, sections, and areas within a store are placed deliberately and with research-level attention. The location of every item in the store has been carefully determined based on assessment of maximum buying power. Some shoppers are expected to come in for one item, find it, and retrace their steps to purchase it and walk out. Therefore, we can understand that stores are going to put those likeliest of single-purchase items squarely in the middle aisles just so single-minded buyers have no choice but to walk past and around tempting items.

Every item, it must be restated, is placed where it is after much calculating and forethought. Venue layouts are fascinatingly sophisticated when it comes to their shelf arrangements. Necessities such as flour, sugar, salt, and spices sit on shelves that are distant from both the entrance and the exit. Unsurprisingly, products displayed at the coveted eye level sell about twice as much as they would anywhere else. Also unsurprisingly, the most expensive items are placed exactly there. Below eye level are the cheaper alternatives. If you take an extra few seconds to look around for desired items, then you won't walk away with what the supermarkets wants you to buy, you walk out with what *you* want to buy. Pay attention to the items that are targeting children at their eye level because the store planners certainly are. Therefore parents often have to resist the adorable pleas of youth when browsing the aisles.

Popular items, such as milk, meats, fish, cheese, and vegetables, can usually be found at the back. While this might also be so that certain food items are as close to the delivery points as possible, we're certain that having shoppers pass almost every other item in the store on the way to these necessities is a happy benefit to sellers. Have you ever walked through a store and thought, *Why is there no space between the aisles or a walkway so that I can cut through to where I want to be?* Well, now you can guess why.

When it comes to shopping for dinnertime, shopping is far from simple. For many of us, cooking is hard work. Preparing fruit and vegetables is time-consuming and laborious. Therefore, it is easy to understand why many of us are looking to make the time spent cooking easier and quicker. For those of us who'd rather spend our free time doing anything but preparing food, stores offer a whole range of processed and prepared food that is much more expensive than their unprepared equivalent, and way unhealthier. It might come as no surprise that these are the items given the best locations and highest visibility throughout stores and supermarkets. Regular fruits and vegetables are much cheaper and better for us but aren't showcased like prepared foods are. Store planners don't only think they know you; they think they know how you *live*. The least you can do is to remind yourself that you know you better than the complete strangers who are selling to you do.

Think online shopping is safer, more predictable? Think again. Websites show more and more often the similar items that other people have bought, in the hope that you put more items into your virtual shopping cart. Think back to how the behavior of others affects everyone else's behavior. It works just as miraculously in the online world. Those of us who have gotten used to shopping at wholesale supermarkets are under the impression that buying bulk-sized products over smaller items will save us money. If we buy an enormous vat of olive oil rather than a small bottle, we think that we are getting a better deal.

Some supermarkets take advantage of our assumption and charge more for the larger quantity than they would for two smaller quantities that combine to equal the same weight as the larger amount. Compare amounts yourself to get the effective price you're paying. It will pay off in the long term, after you have found the cheapest product and keep buying that one repeatedly.

We are also prone to thinking that if we buy more during that shopping trip, we are saving ourselves a trip in the future. However, that reasoning doesn't always hold up because we are more likely to use the items we bought, even in enormous quantity, than save them for later or use them as slowly as we would smaller amounts of the item. Do the math, and don't assume that buying items in bulk is a guaranteed money or time saver.

Finally, we are bombarded by temptation as we pay before leaving. Candy is a seasonal item that sees its highest sales rates around holidays and special occasions. To increase snack and candy sales, these items are deliberately placed by the checkout counter so we see them and buy them on impulse. After all, we have spent time around the sight and smells of so much food, and our appetites are almost always primed, making us susceptible to spend just a little more money than we thought we would. The checkout line is where shoppers are likely to spend time standing and waiting, at our most vulnerable and impatient. The products placed here are often more expensive than those in the main part of the store. Retailers play on your inclination to give in and tell yourself, *Why not? Just one will be okay.*

Shopping for long periods of time means we undergo decision fatigue, which means the brain is tired from making all those little choices, calculations, value judgments, and meal plans while navigating around others. Hungry and tired, most of us can't resist a chocolate bar when we see it as we approach the register. If you want that chocolate bar, then go for it. Remember, you are in control. If you feel that you are being manipulated or taken advantage of, you need not spend any more of your time or money. Have a look at the shopping list you made *before* you went to the store. Did you get everything on there? Then you need not ponder purchases of further items. You made it. Congratulations!

* * *

Gathering news is a lot like gathering groceries. In a world that is eager to get you riled up about so much information that might not impact your life, it pays to know who you are before others rush to decide that for you. Determining if you, on any given day, have only enough time to look into local news, have time to get the spread on world headlines, want to know what is breaking on the cutting edge of technology, or are bothered just with last night's sports results is key to effectively knowing what news applies to you.

Back when newspapers were all the rage, it was easy to flip to the section you wanted to know more about and ignore everything that didn't matter to you. You could target the local points of interest, the sports section, the financial pages, whatever you wanted without being obligated to read through the rest. Reading the news meant not having to listen to sponsors, not being emotionally manipulated by music or raised dopamine levels, and being better able to digest the news on our own terms. It must have been a quieter and simpler process—much easier to keep our senses amid the wide world of information than it is keeping informed through televised news reports. The moment we turn on the news channel, we are swept into an ever-moving current of conversations, images, videos, clips, and voices that assure us how important it is that we stay tuned to know more about whatever it is being discussed that very moment.

This isn't an accident.

It has been said that those who tell the stories rule the world, and most stories argue for what is thought to be the most moral to the storyteller. Storytelling is an excellent way to capture people's attention, imprint information into their minds, and create undeniably personal bonds, even between enemies or among strangers. People crave great stories almost as often as they crave food, shelter, and sex. Those who learn how to tell the most compelling stories can command the most influence within their social group and learn how to acquire respect among their peers. The most powerful way to keep audiences paying attention to a story is to use certain tried-and-true narrative techniques. In short, no one can resist a good story told well. The news is broadcast in a way that reflects this, and it does so to keep viewer attention long enough to warm viewers to a certain mindset, push a particular agenda, and expose people to what their sponsors are selling.

Watching the news requires the viewer to navigate through editorial selections, as well as through visual and audio elements, in a particular order that has been carefully directed. This direction may not be to intervene, create bias, or spread falsehoods, even though it can easily do these things through the compelling narrative structure. News stories integrate multiple cultural, historical, and economic factors, then normalize such factors through perceived voices of authority and cyclical repetition. Ideology is a sense of culturally specific beliefs about the world that are usually absorbed and taken for granted. Through the narrative process, people on the television and internet are able to do more than just pass along the news of the day; they are able to build and reinforce ideologies that others are inevitably going to want to popularize. Satellites, a wide selection of television channels, and the ubiquity of the internet allow more people than ever before to choose from news services that might have originally been made for a very different audience with a very different ideology. Conflicting ideologies can produce multiple perspectives on a given fact, report, or ongoing event.

Audiences may not be aware that the way news is delivered varies quite drastically depending on who they are and what they, as listeners, impart to the story. There are news outlets that tailor their information deliveries for liberals, conservatives, wealthy people, the struggling class, citizens, refugees, followers of religion, and secular progressives. Trigger words, veiled accusations, and factual-sounding opinions are lightly dusted among defensible and harmless facts so that listeners are made to not just learn about what is going on but also *feel* things about what is going on. People are subliminally invited to bring their own experiences to the information they are presented with and guided to arrive at certain opinions and conclusions much the same way a shopper is guided past tempting luxuries on their way to get the milk.

Conflict, tragedy, and natural disasters must be presented as having great significance to the listeners and their lives. The closer the event or story is to the intended audience, the more likely it is to gain our attention and affect our behaviors. Most of the time, journalists must tell the news in a way that makes it relevant, or interesting, through narrative structure, principles, trust, and implication. The thing that makes the news the news is that, since way back, it has been seen to champion professional values, namely objectivity, legitimacy, integrity, and impartiality. These values are often upheld by institutional professional standards, but for those agencies that might not cherish such values, there are rules demanding that news sources adhere to these values. These values are considered of special importance in hard news, which reports on all that is considered to influence the world's citizens. On the other hand, entertainment news, opinion pieces, and other soft news covers stories that have to do with celebrity, crime, and domestic affairs. Soft news is typically written according to narrative devices, while hard news conforms to a construct called the inverted pyramid.

The inverted pyramid ensures that the most important information will be read to and clarified for the audience first. This means that the most important information in the story is summarized in the beginning of the broadcast, usually with the lead sentence. Standard practice has the lead sentence answer the five Ws: who, what, when, where, and why. The story talks about important factors, such as timeliness, prominence, consequence, proximity, conflict, et cetera, in order of importance. The inverted pyramid is also a reliable model for news storytelling specifically because it conceals government views with objective reporting. The inverted pyramid pleases a public audience that generally prefers a more concise style that is easy to comprehend, while also saving newspaper publishers expensive distribution costs. To maximize sales and readership appeal, news agencies came to report the news as objectively as possible, without the risk of alienating any dissenting political or philosophical opinions.

In certain news programs, the opinionating and speculative soft news format is presented as the more authentic hard news format, which convinces some of the news-watching audience to digest opinions and unfounded statements as facts to take to heart.

The inverted pyramid construction continues to permeate televised news writing because it emphasizes information over speculation or hyperbole. However, news sources have discovered that they acquire greater viewership by integrating a style that warms the relationship between the broadcaster and the news watching audience. As a result the journalistic ideals of detachment and objectivity have taken on, over time, a more engaged style of journalism. Therefore, the journalist continues to enhance the story experience, always motivated to keep the audience engaged in ways that deepen the relationship between news and audiences more than ever before. NBC executive Reuven Frank vocalized this idea in a 1963 memo to his news team: "Every news story should, without any sacrifice of probity or responsibility, display the attributes of fiction, of drama. It should have structure and conflict, problem and denouement, rising action and falling action, a beginning, a middle and an end. These are not only the essentials of drama; they are the essentials of narrative."

We may not necessarily agree with such a statement, but if it is this statement that influences our future journalists, then we should watch and read news carefully, with a grain of salt. In the language of news journalism, a story is a factual account of events. The same classical narrative that gives flow to memoirs, fiction, and Hollywood movies contains a number of features that are notably absent from traditionally constructed, inverted pyramid news stories, such as sequential development, cause-effect relationships, a double chronology of narrated time and the time of the events narrated, resolution, and closure. The reporter continues to be represented as an authoritative and reliable storyteller, perpetuating the inherent legitimacy that characterizes newscasters.

Opening sequences usually employ visual symbols such as a revolving globe or a ticking clock to establish urgency and immediacy. Typically the whole opening sequence ends in the professional space of the studio. In the studio we find the newsreaders behind desks, formally dressed, and with a businesslike demeanor. Using two newsreaders makes dialogue and conversation easier to coordinate, especially when moving between more serious and lighter items. It appeals to the audience's humanity and makes us lean in and empathize more than we would if the news anchors were merely briefing us on the news. The mode of address, plus the relations of copresence, encourages the audience's agreement, almost to a level of endearment.

News anchors use tried and true conventions of narration to coordinate with the images and sounds that accompany a news story. A slew of techniques goes into establishing the legitimacy of the news so effectively that it discourages viewers from questioning certain narratives. Like other shows on television, the media is well placed to show people a certain view of the world and filter current events through a particular bias that influences how reality is perceived. As a result we are subliminally led to think that the newsreader is speaking to us and for us. The broadcasts persuade the viewers to see the significance of events for themselves, with an almost imperceptible nudge.

It can be difficult to keep our heads when so much is placed directly in our field of vision with such authority, making it almost impossible to see anything else. The authoritative look of the newsreader is yet another trick to make us believe and trust. Scientists have shown that people tend to follow more blindly someone who looks like a figure of authority. Sometimes all it takes is a white doctor's overall or a neat suit to make us believe and trust in the person we're seeing and who is talking to us. It's comparable to the eye-level shelves in a supermarket and all the beautifully designed packaging and branding of the products laid out on those shelves.

News broadcasts employ the most successful storytelling techniques and put them to effective use in a process akin to welcoming wanderers into a well-signposted maze. The opening sequence of a broadcast or news segment—usually a call to attention—serves as an interruption to the flow of entertainment programming to capture viewer interest, with bright colors and a fanfare-like theme. They even use music to their advantage. This catches the mind like a basket of hot and fresh baguettes, and we can't help but want to eat it all up.

Don't abstain from being informed. If all the news you can access is televised media, be mindful that it may be soft news that you are watching. Further, keep in mind that the entire news broadcast is a story designed to hold your interest at best and to lead you to certain conclusions about world events in more and more instances. Without shared myths and stories, society loses meaning. Without meaning, cultures risk extinction. Truth is the best adhesive to strengthen our stories, making them last so we can weave them well over time, enriching our cultural identity. If you keep your head, you can take note of the facts and frame without having to conform to someone else's context. Remember, *you* are in control. If you feel that you are being manipulated or taken advantage of, you need not give a news story your trust if you don't feel it has earned it. We are fortunate to have so many different news resources at our fingertips: the internet-age allows you to follow up on everything, to review, to read or watch more. Don't be surprised if on another media channel you suddenly find the exact opposite of what you've been taught on your primary media channel.

IV
Reading the Fine Print

*Words used carelessly, as if they did not matter
in any serious way, often allowed otherwise
well-guarded truths to seep through.*

—Douglas Adams,
The Long Dark Tea-Time of the Soul

Successful communication is important, especially for those of us who want to know what we are buying and, by extension, eating. Knowing what we are buying makes us more mindful shoppers, more economical spenders, and healthier people. Awareness of ingredients is a big stepping-stone toward achieving health goals. We usually determine how healthy an item in the store is by what we learned growing up from parents, what the package says, and where it is in the store. Most of the time, when we shop for groceries, we're either too exhausted, too hurried, or too hungry to take the time to thoroughly read the labels before putting an item in the shopping basket. It's also easy to grab familiar foods without thinking twice, never suspecting that they might not be good for us or have it occur to us that the ingredients have changed over time.

With so many foods to choose from—and so much confusing information and language, even misinformation, on labels—it is almost impossible to make informed choices with confidence without extra research. All of this makes it even more difficult to identify ingredients that we might want to reduce to keep a heart-healthy diet, such as saturated and trans fats, sodium, added sugars, and cholesterol. Most consumers around the world are becoming more health-conscious, so a lot of grocery manufacturers are using more misleading tactics to convince people like you and us to purchase highly processed and unhealthy products.

Even if we know exactly what we're looking for, and even when there is enough time to examine and compare items, reading labels can be tricky, and it's easy to become overwhelmed. We have no idea what most of those huge words mean. A lot of the time, we have no clue if something has a lot of sugar, not to mention sodium and trans fats.

Food labeling regulations are complex, adding to the difficulty for consumers of understanding them. One of the best tips may be to completely ignore claims on food packaging. Labels try to lure consumers into purchasing products by making broad health claims that make us feel safe and confident in buying them. In fact, research shows that adding health claims to front labels makes people believe a product is healthier than the same product that doesn't list health claims. But know this:

manufacturers are often dishonest in their labeling. It's almost like a law or rule in marketing groceries to make labels imply that products are healthier for us than they really are. Most of us would walk out of the store with a bottle of candy if it looked like vitamins, and we'd be none the wiser.

Now more than ever, it is important for consumers to choose healthy options by reading thoroughly the ingredients list to keep from becoming prey to pretty packages and beautiful words that only end up improving our feelings, not our bodies. When they are listed, product ingredients are listed from highest to lowest quantity. A good rule of thumb is to scan the first three ingredients as they make up the largest part of what you're eating. The first ingredient is what the manufacturer used the most of. If the first ingredients include refined grains, a type of sugar, or hydrogenated oils, the product is unhealthy. Healthy products have whole foods listed as the first three ingredients. In addition, an ingredients list that is longer than two to three lines suggests that the product is highly processed. "Processed" foods are nutritionally inferior to unprocessed foods. They generally include packaged food items containing many hard-to-pronounce ingredients. They also usually contain artificial colors, flavors, and other chemical additives. Often referred to as convenience or preprepared foods, processed foods are suggested to be a contributor to the obesity epidemic and rising prevalence of chronic diseases like heart disease and diabetes.

Food labels, if they are responsible, state how many calories and nutrients are in a standard amount of the product, usually as a suggested single serving. We can have a hard time believing what is deemed a serving size, especially after a workout. These serving sizes are often much smaller than what people like us consume in one sitting. Who would suspect that one serving might be only half a can of soda, a quarter of a chocolate chip cookie, half a chocolate bar, or a single bagel? Hungry eaters who don't look at the labels are unaware of this serving size measurement, while the hopeful dare to think the entire container is a single serving. With small serving size measurements, manufacturers get to list smaller numbers in the calorie category, which is what most consumers, including us, only really look at most of the time.

Health claims on packaged food are prominent and meant to catch shoppers' attention and convince us that the product is healthy for us. Often we will find claims like "low fat," "reduced salt," or "high fiber" on the labels and packaging, persuading us to select that product. However, while nutrition content claims can generally lead us to make healthier choices, it is upon us to know what these claims mean, not just the words themselves. This means we must verify claims on labels by looking at the product nutrition information. A few words in particular are highlighted for interest because they are used so often, all over the world, but might not always mean the same thing we think they do.

If a product is called "light," it means that it is processed to reduce either calories or fat. It should be emphasized here that reduced fat and low-fat do not mean the same thing. Here's an example: "Low-fat" means that something has 3g or less fat per 100g (i.e., 3 percent fat), while "reduced fat" means a product is 25 per cent lower in fat than what the product usually contains. Many times, such foods start off as very high in fat, for example mayonnaise, potato chips, and cheese, so that they can be repackaged as healthier products later under the illusion of being made healthy or guilt-free. If a food that starts with 50 percent fat and has 25 percent reduced fat, this really means that now the new, "light" version still has 37.5 percent fat. Over a third of the product is pure fat!

"Multigrain" makes most of us feel like the product that bears this description is filled with an array of vitamins and nourishment like the foods of old, without synthetic additives, while multigrain in fact only means that it contains more than one type of grain. Unless the product is marked as "whole grain," the grains that are used in making these products are most likely refined grains. "Refined" refers to grain products that consist of grains or flours that have been greatly modified from their natural state by removing nutritious brans and germs, either through grinding or selective sifting. Similarly, "natural" does not necessarily mean that a certain product is pure from the earth, untouched by synthetic processes. In the food production industry, the word "natural" only means that at some point in the manufacturing process, the manufacturer used a natural source, like apples, grain, or rice. Just because a label states that it was "made with whole grains" doesn't mean it offers the wide array of hearty vitamins that comes to most peoples' minds. It may, in most cases, offer very few whole grains. This is where checking the ingredient list helps us out. If whole grains aren't in the first three ingredients, then there probably aren't enough whole grain nutrients to get excited about.

If something is "fortified or enriched," it means that some nutrients have been added to the product. However, the fact that something is fortified doesn't mean it is any healthier than it would be otherwise. For example, vitamin D is often added to milk, but that doesn't mean that the unhealthy side effects of milk are any less harmful if consumed in excess. According to the rules used by the food industry, one could say that chocolate cake is fortified with frosting or that cocaine is fortified with regret.

In much the same way as other healthy-sounding claims, "gluten-free" doesn't mean that products are made better by recent science, only that the products don't contain wheat, spelt, rye, or barley. Therefore, a lot of gluten-free foods are highly processed, which means that they are loaded with unhealthy fats and sugar. Most of us already know this, but it can be easy to forget that "fruit-flavored" products might not contain any fruit, just chemicals added so that products look and taste like fruit. If something is labeled "zero trans fat," it means that there are less than 0.5 grams of trans fat per serving, as opposed to none. If serving sizes are misleadingly small, as they so often are, there is going to be at least some trans fat in a "zero trans fat" product.

Most of us are under the impression that fat, in and of itself, has nothing good, and that it should be avoided as much as possible. Manufacturers know this, and tailor language around fat that persuades us to get foods that have much unhealthier ingredients that are used in order to appeal to our tastes and senses. "Low-fat" makes us think there is merely a low amount of fat in the product, but it also usually means that the manufacturer has added more sugar so the fat can be reduced. This is where it pays for us, as shoppers, to read and understand the list of ingredients.

A lot of people try to eat fewer carbohydrates in order to lose weight and slim down. Many people entertain low-carb diets by avoiding pasta and bread, even though dairy, fruit, and vegetables are also naturally occurring carbohydrates. We love broccoli, so that means we love eating carbs. It pays to know that carbohydrates are macronutrients, just like proteins and fats, so they are a contributing part of every person's overall health. We can forgive people for wanting to look after their bodies, so it's worth bringing to light that "low-carb" processed foods are still processed junk foods, just like processed low-fat foods.

We all have been told repeatedly, since we were children, that sugar isn't something that we need to consume huge amounts of and that we should avoid overdoing. We know that sugar gives us energy, tastes good, and when consumed in excess, will cause heart disease and make us unhealthy. It comes as no surprise that many food manufacturers dance around when coming clean with how much sugar is in their products and tell us this data in language that makes us feel okay about consuming their products. Phrases like "no added sugar" don't mean there isn't much sugar inside; they only mean that sugar substitutes, many of which can be worse than actual sugar, may have been added. Most of us know only enough about calories to know that we should be mindful of them and not consume too many, so it pays to know that when a food is labeled as "low-calorie," it only means that there are fewer calories than in the brand's original product.

Those of us who want to stay on top of our sugar consumption should check food labels carefully to see if anything special has been added. Sugar goes by many names that most of us may not recognize. Food manufacturers use this to their advantage by purposely adding many different types of sugar to their products to hide the total sugar amount. By doing this, manufacturers can list a healthier ingredient at the top. This way, even a product loaded with sugar may not have it listed as one of the top three ingredients. Keep a look out for beet sugar, brown sugar, buttered sugar, cane sugar, caster sugar, coconut sugar, date sugar, golden sugar, invert sugar, muscovado sugar, organic raw sugar, raspadura sugar, evaporated cane juice, and confectioner's sugar. In addition, these sugary sources are worth making note of when calculating total sugars: carob syrup, golden syrup, high-fructose corn syrup, honey, agave nectar, malt syrup, maple syrup, oat syrup, rice bran syrup, and rice syrup. Other added sugars used in products might include barley malt, molasses, cane juice crystals, lactose, corn sweetener, crystalline fructose, dextran, malt powder, ethyl maltol, fructose, fruit juice concentrate, galactose, glucose, disaccharides, maltodextrin, and maltose. Quite daunting, isn't it? Many more names for sugar exist, but these are the most common. Without doing research, we would have never known that all these ingredients meant sugar, and we might never have even paid attention to them. From now on, if we see any of these in the top spots on the ingredients lists, we'll know that the product is high in added sugar, no matter what names it goes under. A final suggestion on this matter: no matter what name it goes under, sugar is always still sugar. Our body absorbs and transforms all the previously mentioned ingredients to the same one thing: sugar.

The term "organic" is also used descriptively for an action, like "I try to live organically" or "Organic farming is better for the planet." Some popular retailers set their own standards for what they'll sell with an organic label. Still, just because a label makes certain claims doesn't guarantee that it's healthy. Certain foods produced organically are not nutritionally superior to foods produced scientifically. Organic produce may cost less at farmers markets because of lower shipping costs, but it can be difficult to know what you're getting. If you want to know for certain if something is organic or not, it helps to know that farmers who market their products as organic are supposed to have their organic certification paperwork. Vendors are supposed to have it on hand if they are selling organic food items, textiles, toys, furniture, mattresses, cosmetics, beverages, bath and body care products, and other products.

Despite all these attempts to mislead the shopping public, there are healthy foods out there that are organic, whole grain, and natural. If we have a sweet tooth or love a great cheese with a sumptuous glass (or bottle) of wine, we can happily indulge in a healthy amount. Enjoying foods and beverages with upfront integrity is better than laboring under the illusion that we are perfectly healthy. An occasional little treat helps us to be more diligent for longer periods of time and make sound choices when we go shopping.

* * *

If knowing what certain words mean in the store can help us to nourish our bodies more effectively, we think that knowing the exact meaning of words that the media likes to use can help us to nourish our minds and philosophies better. The media plays about as fast and loose with words that get viewers riled up as food manufacturers do. A working knowledge of certain keywords can go a long way toward helping us, as viewers, keep our heads.

Capitalism is the economic system by which a country's trade, industry, and profits are controlled by private companies, instead of by the people whose time and labor powers those companies. Supporters of capitalism argue that the desire for profit incentivizes people and corporations to innovate, improve systems, and develop new products that will be met with sufficient demand. It is argued that without the motivation to earn, management, workers, and developers are unlikely to make the effort required to produce new ideas or products.

In a capitalist economic system, the government (state) does not directly employ the workforce. This lack of government-run employment can lead to unemployment during economic struggles. To overcome flaws and struggles, capitalist societies acknowledge certain obligations. Obligations include the mitigation of poverty, the improvement of public health, and the enhancement of individual quality of life.

The proper role of government in a capitalist economic system has been hotly debated for centuries. While nearly all economic thinkers and policymakers argue in favor of some level of government influence in the capitalist economy, most discussions of power in natural resource management tend to omit the primary issue of capitalism, which is how we utilize and manage resources in a way that rewards participation and effort. Any economy is capitalist as long as private individuals, as opposed to the state, control the factors of production. However, just because a system is regulated by the government doesn't mean it isn't a capitalist economy as the profits of capitalist endeavors can, and often are, subject to taxation. It makes sense to us that in order to create a more ethical capitalist system, capitalist societies should continue to integrate more compassionate values and ethics into economic systems.

Communism is an economic system where the government owns and directs the systems of production and allocates resources. Karl Marx and Friedrich Engels popularized the communist system as a means to end the exploitation of the masses by the few. At the time these philosophers saw that capitalist systems required people to work under harsh and dangerous conditions for little pay. Desiring to create a system that improved the quality of life of citizens, communism was designed to eliminate class distinctions so that citizens could share in the proceeds of society on a more equal trajectory: "from each according to his abilities, to each according to his needs."

Marx and Engels perceived a struggle between the classes over matters of labor, means of production, land, raw materials, tools, and money. Although Marx and Engels believed that property should belong to society, the government was determined to own society's means of production, which should be managed by employees of the state. Economic resources were devoted to industrialization and the military, which sometimes resulted in intense competition for consumer goods. As a response to this competition, communist economies emphasized a culture's self-reliance.

Supporters of the communist ideology champion the widespread universal social welfare that the system promises. Public health and education, provision of childcare, provision of state-directed social services, and provision of social benefits will, unobstructed by mismanagement and other human failings, help to raise productivity and social developments. Communist ideology also advocates universal education and supports the equal treatment of all people, regardless of education, status, or personal wealth. Because the government owns all means of production, the government can theoretically provide jobs for the people who want them. In a communist economy, work opportunities, pay, and other work benefits are offered to every citizen who fulfills their part. Theoretically, if the government dictates economic structure, economic instability is out of the question. Every citizen is required to work in order to receive benefits, and those who don't experience corresponding sanctions. This creates an incentive to participate and to encourage economic growth. In communist societies everyone can work harmoniously without stepping on each other's toes. Work, responsibility, and rewards are meant to be shared among the citizens.

Because only authorized dissent is allowed in the communist context, people who feel like their voices are not being heard tend to resort to violence or violent rhetoric to make their point. If people develop a sense of envy, jealousy, or cultivate ambitions that go against the goals of the state, then a harmonious economic development can't come to fruition. Only absolute cooperation allows for effective and equal resource distribution. When workers sense that they are being taken advantage of by their fellow citizens or by their government, the likelihood of terrorism increases. If terrorism increases, governmental responses to threats escalate and become more ferocious. Secret police and other forms of enforcement are then used to maintain control within the governmental structure. The structure is easy to manipulate for government officials because only one entity has oversight over everything in the society. One politician can tweak the rules and laws so that their class of people receive the most compensation while still mandating everyone else to work for virtually nothing. Communism might have the goal of uplifting everyone in a society, but mismanaged resources and an absence of compassion can result in greed, poverty, and death.

The definition of socialism can vary widely, but it can be safely distinguished as an economic system somewhere between communism and capitalism. Supporters of socialism and mixed economies champion the benefits of everyone equally owning the factors of production that have been acquired through a democratically elected government. Socialists consider both individual needs and greater social needs when allocating resources through addressing needs of transportation, defense, education, health care, and preservation of natural resources, as well as caring for those who can't directly contribute to production. A sense of compassion motivates socialists to work overtime when situations ask it of them, and workers receive their share of resources after a percentage has been deducted for the common good. Socialists believe that the basic nature of people is cooperative and that this basic nature hasn't yet emerged in full because most economic systems force people to be competitive. Socialists argue that the best economic system must support this basic human nature so that compassionate human qualities can discover their fullest expression.

People who are unfamiliar with, or misrepresent, socialism argue against public ownership and plead for private control of property and natural resources. Socialists argue that since everyone contributes to society in the form of work, everyone should benefit from it. Socialism covers many varying philosophies and opinions about ownership and control of resource distribution. Some believe that the government should own most of the property and natural resources, while others believe that small businesses entities should be owned privately. Unlike communists, most socialists do not advocate violence or force to achieve their economic system. This is because under socialism, workers aren't harshly exploited because they own the means of production. Profits are spread equitably among all workers according to their individual contribution, and the cooperative system also provides for those who can't work. The system yearns to meet basic needs for the whole society, providing equal access to health care and education, discriminating against no one.

People are suspicious of socialist systems because socialist governments have enormous power, and such governments are only beneficial if they represent the wishes of the people. Socialism gets a lot of resistance from those who are against the idea of redistributing wealth and communal ownership of natural resources, major industries, and public utilities. Commonly, government leaders abuse this privilege by taking power for themselves. A disadvantage of socialism is that it relies on the cooperative nature of humans and depends on people to work together unselfishly, honestly, and for the greater good of all. Most people are capable of this kind of compassion, but they aren't willing to trust others to comply. Ambitious people tend to seek ways to disrupt society for their own gain. Capitalism harnesses this ambition as a "greed is good" mantra, while socialism pretends greed is unimportant or can be minimized. As a result, socialism doesn't reward people for being entrepreneurial and struggles to be as innovative as a capitalistic society. However, there tends to be a stronger safety net in socialist systems for workers who are injured or in need of help.

A mixed economy solution respects multiple political philosophies and gets to take advantage of the best of all ideas. For example, respecting private property rights but placing limits on them qualifies as a mixed economy based on multiple philosophies. Some people might balk at the idea of looking at systems or political philosophies beyond the one they were born into, but we don't think it's sensible of us to ignore or criticize a system on the mere basis of what we've been told in passing or witnessed in a few well-broadcasted flaws, courtesy of a media that is all too eager to guide our convictions. We tend to think that selecting from a series of competing systems, all of which flourish and flounder in varying degrees, is an idea that benefits all cultures and communities. We think it behooves us as citizens to look at various political philosophies and see what works and what doesn't work when it comes to resource allocation and world needs. If we only embrace systems that have come before under the guise of country pride, what social growth can society reasonably expect? Rather than argue for one system or another as if they were sports teams that benefitted from our dedication and allegiance, we could adopt a smarter and more mature mindset.

After going through some of the ways that people have tried to agree on control and expenditure of the world's resources, it may be worth it to see how people assemble to conduct themselves. These terms of collectivism are often misunderstood and used effectively to galvanize people for and against political ideas all the time.

Democracy concerns decision-making that is made for different kinds of groups such as families, voluntary organizations, economic firms, diplomatic states, and global organizations. The equality required by a democracy may be the formal equality of one-person one-vote, or it may be expressed through the processes of coalition building and other political arrangements. This can include direct participation of individuals to determine laws and policies, or it may involve designated representatives making the decisions. Democracy is thought to be more reliable in helping participants discover the right decisions because it invites the masses into the decision-making process. In this way democratic processes can take advantage of multiple sources of information, as well as consider criticisms of said policies without fear of punishment. Democratic decision-making tends to be more informed than many other forms, especially when it comes to the interests of average citizens and the policies being considered to advance those interests. Some people argue that democracy may not be the best decision-making system, however, because citizens may not all be optimally informed about politics and policies that dominate the headlines. This unfamiliarity can lead to a public that is apathetic and results in low participation in the citizenry. When citizens believe that their voices have no effect, they allow special interests to control politicians and their agendas.

Meritocracy is described as a system that rewards merit (ability combined with effort) with success. A system that rewards people by merit is thought to encourage individual and collective effort. When rewards are tied to one's abilities and achievements, people are motivated to strive and be the best they can be. This might seem like a good system, but let's consider a few things first. If rewards are tied to unearned qualities, like inherited wealth, social connections, or race, behaviors might change in morally hazardous ways. Social corruption increases if people are encouraged to hoard resources that benefit themselves and their families while taking away from the rest of society.

A meritocracy that measures people on wealth and privilege, as opposed to performance itself, is likely to be wasteful and suboptimal. When one person's success depends on them outperforming others, that person has no incentive to help others succeed. A system that allocates rewards based on relative performance is likely to reduce trust and cooperation. There is no reason to expect those who have succeeded in a meritocracy to direct their energies toward socially beneficial activities. Some forms of meritocracy suggest that subsiding and extending tax breaks to the rich helps the wealthy class to create jobs and prosperity for the rest, while other forms of meritocracy suggest that fiscal policies should ensure that the public can afford basic needs. This means that wealth redistribution and social policies guarantee housing and health care, retirement security, and protection against involuntary unemployment to everyone, to reduce inequality.

Oligarchy comes from the Greek word *oligarkhes*, which means "rule of the few." Any system can become an oligarchy if power becomes concentrated in the hands of a few very wealthy and privileged people. In a monarchy or tyranny, they have enough power and money to influence the king or tyrant. In a democracy oligarchs use their relationships and money to influence the elected officials. Power is usually delegated to a group of experts so that an organization can function because it's inefficient for everyone to make all the decisions all the time.

This way, most people can focus on their day-to-day lives and ignore the issues that concern society. They can spend their time doing other things, such as working on their chosen career, cultivating relationships with their families, or writing books about how supermarket manipulations are a lot like media political narratives.

After enough accumulation of resources at the expense of others, the growing oligarchy becomes an extreme form of aristocracy, in which power is vested in a hereditary group set apart from the rest of society by religion, kinship, economic status, prestige, or even language to concentrate power within their own class, and so the oligarchical class becomes an organized minority, making it difficult for the average person to enter the group of elites. In this way, oligarchs' power and wealth can increase over time as they make laws designed to favor themselves unbeknownst to the general citizenry. It can be easy for a ruling class, left unchecked, to manipulate financial markets to their advantage to acquire even more wealth and power. Oligarchies increase income inequality as the ruling caste leaves less for most everyone else and seeks to keep their power. When the general public loses the hope that they can join the oligarchy through hard work and well-developed skills, this disrupts the social structure, harms the economy, and causes pain and suffering for all.

The words misused by the media, political speakers, and people with loud opinions are many and almost endless. Hopefully, more and more people can take the time to remember the awesome power of words. The importance of remembering what emotionally loaded words mean can help us to not just know more about the groceries we are putting in our shopping carts but also more about the thoughts we are putting inside our heads.

V
That's Entertainment!

Anyone who tries to make a distinction between education and entertainment doesn't know the first thing about either.

—Marshall McLuhan

For some people, shopping is a chore. For others, shopping is a the best way to spend a weekend. At certain times, in certain situations, and with certain people, shopping can be a stress buster and a welcome form of entertainment. Much more than just a way to acquire goods, produce, and resources, shopping can often be a source of happiness, especially when people shop with, or for, someone special. When people become overwhelmed by life but aren't free to drink deeply from the well of adventure or travel, shopping diverts the mind and keeps people engrossed. Some shoppers like the break from routine and take the opportunity to show off their clothes, meet up with friends, see what new technology exists, and discover tempting deals for things that might otherwise be out of their grasp.

Shops know this and are all about fusing retail and entertainment to bedazzle and impress shoppers immediately. Shoppers are drawn into stores with warm hues, such as reds, oranges, and yellows. Cool interior colors, such as blues and greens, encourage shoppers to spend more. The packaging on premium brands is specifically designed to tempt us into spending extra, but the extra cash only gets that fancy packaging. That "high quality," more expensive ground turkey looks nicer than the cheaper stuff, but can we really taste the difference, or do we just think we can? A loaf of bread and a pint of milk by themselves can look odd all alone in a big shopping cart, so shoppers are subliminally led to fill the cart with other things to fill up more of the cart space. Shopping carts have almost tripled in size over time, persuading customers to purchase more per visit.

Shop designers set up spectacles or attractions to grab the attention of shoppers. In some cases, shops include celebrities or industry professionals to attract people with something they don't see every day. Indulgent shoppers are looking to be attracted to new products and are more likely to choose chocolate over vegetables, the sports car over the sensible family-friendly vehicle. These shoppers are happy to spend more for branded products and might spend money on a whim, whatever seems good at the time. We look for excitement and let ourselves engage with the story behind the product. This goes double for when we develop an emotional connection to the brand or product.

It is worth remembering, as a shopper, that retailers operate on the theory that the quickest way to our credit cards is through our senses. Some stores flood our perceptions with atmospherics designed to entice us so that we linger for a longer time and spend more, based on what they, and psychologists, know about us. We either make purchases based on our preference for a brand name, or we buy the things we do to align with the image we perceive the product to represent. In general, we'll make smarter purchases if we are aware of our own shopping temperaments. Any type of emotional or physical strain can impair your judgement. Just as we are going to buy differently on an empty stomach than we would with a full belly, if we're down, we will make different buying decisions than when we shop with a happy mind. If shopping is something you do to cheer yourself up, then do it. It may be helpful to set a budget to avoid being ruled by impulses, just as it might behoove shoppers to eat before going food shopping.

Researching everything there is to know about stores and products helps to minimize some of the emotional bombardment that impulsive customers revel in. But even the most resilient, skeptical, and thoughtful shoppers can be persuaded to change their decisions with the right nudge and in the right settings. Decisions can change if shoppers provide sellers with certain information, allowing retailers to cater their stores and presentations so that shoppers find greater peace of mind. In this way, sellers and retailers lure shoppers with reviews, guides, and anything else they can dream of to convince shoppers to purchase from them and by offering products that are what shoppers have in mind.

If you are feeling low, and you know it will lift your spirits, go shop. Just know that during emotional lows you are more likely to buy unnecessary items because we are chasing that dopamine rush that comes with buying something new. There are times when we give ourselves over to the shopping experience because we have some time to kill or we're interested in seeing what new products a certain store has that season. We can always count on being entertained, but we know how to maintain control of our behaviors (most of the time). If we're following a budget, knowing how much we want to spend before we go shopping allows us to resist the urge to overspend. Whether we're only looking for particular items or we're looking to spend an afternoon browsing, we set an amount for ourselves. Boundaries are good! When the cash runs out, our purchasing power is reached, and we refuse to use our credit cards. Knowing which shops we're going to go to helps us to make sure we don't forget anything and keeps us somewhat prepared for the spectacle of products that are sure to impress us once we walk in the mall or supermarket. Keeping our heads when we're pressured to spend money and time makes the entertainment of shopping something not to be dreaded but enjoyed.

* * *

For some people, engaging the mediascape for information is a chore. For some, navigating through sources to see the world's events is a fun time. With each passing decade, people are consuming mass quantities of news in strange contexts. While the news vehicles are conveniently catered to our preferences, schedules, and whims, vested parties exercise sweeping freedoms to market the news delivery so that audiences are drawn to them.

Journalists, publishers, and others have always played with our news so that audiences can access the news imaginatively and in wider contexts than the generation before. Paying attention to the news hasn't been just a tallying of events for a long time, if it ever was. Historically the presentation of information and events has deliberately favored rulers and politicians who are privileged and able to influence headlines. Audiences are compelled to know about people who command respect and fear, even if there is no public acquisition of genuine information. The difference between news and entertainment has all but been erased so that it's almost impossible to tell reporters from entertainers.

The tension between journalism and commercialism goes back long before visual media, but it has risen to inconceivable heights. In the first days of televised news, when a newscaster expressed an opinion, it came with a disclaimer. As the news mixed with politics, the legitimacy of the news started to become less authentic. To get people to watch the news, broadcasters had to make the program less of a briefing and more of a feature. In this way, those who brought news to the masses started to mix the seriousness of raw information with entertainment to keep people engaged.

We tend to like candy when we're sad, familiar songs when we're traveling, and good humor when our spirits are low. Entertainment and comedy are good bedfellows. Comedy has been a great way to vent frustration and other negative feelings brought on by despair, expectations of society, and our inability to change what we want in the world.

Consultants to media industries emphasize entertainment values. This kind of effort to prioritize attractiveness over authenticity of content seems to be more pervasive with each passing year. The results are that news formats center on crime, disaster, perceived slights, and human interest stories. The content of the stories may or may not be relevant to the audience, but they are made irresistible to us by intrigue and distraction. Political comedy projects coolness and youth and is popular among audiences who are disillusioned by experts, journalists, and politicians. Many of the tools that online newsmakers use are considered playful. Politicians discovered that it may be even more beneficial to bypass conventions and gatekeepers of mass media, like editors, moderators, producers. This way, the powerful can speak directly to the multitudes through various platforms and directly to their target demographic, the same way that a stand-up comedian might.

The overlapping of news and entertainment influences viewers like us. We used to assume that we could trust what we were told, probably because the speakers were dressed with authority and the screen was surrounded with official-sounding music and friendly banners. The newsroom-like sets with monitors and entertainers wearing business attire go a long way toward making viewers take them, their opinions, and their agendas as seriously as they would a legitimate news source. The content has no official or journalistic substance, and these sources present nothing new in the way of actual truth at all. The illusion of competence and legitimacy has spilled into almost every media market and form of communication, with effective results. The pretense to uphold unbiased information while continuing to appeal to audience emotions leads to massive viewership and widespread success in spreading almost imperceptible messaging. Through well-chosen language and wearing a cloak of shared ideals, anyone who can master the irresistibly entertaining gleam of professionalism is free to broadcast whatever agenda they want, subtly knitted into their communications. Sometimes news stories are relevant and bereft of a shifting agenda, designed only to direct viewer attention toward meaningful stories. These pure reports, however, may be peppered in between opinion pieces to provide structure for surrounding entertainment segments. The overall narrative, then, combines information, misinformation, and even disinformation at times while being presented as fact to the untrained eye.

At any given time, a person is presented information by a mix of satirical posts, trending stories, catchy headlines, and interesting news. Some media outlets use comedy more and more in order to rise above the rest and be seen and heard better. A story that can employ entertainment through making people laugh at the world around them doesn't only get noticed but also often helps lead viewers to intelligent insights. Funny political news and commentary, satirized reporting, and weird news stories from real life are just as relevant to current events and areas of public interest as any scholarly presentation or news broadcast. Just because something makes us laugh doesn't mean we can't also take it seriously. There are hilarious articles about world events that we can relate to better than what is talked about in headline news, so it is worth noticing the formats and practices by which news and opinions are disseminated. As industries and the powers that be adapt to compete for attention, like products in a supermarket, it shouldn't surprise us that legitimate sources are taking a more playful attitude to giving us the news, just as illegitimate propaganda takes steps to appear authentic, to be taken as fact.

The selection of relevant, and irrelevant, subjects that the media draws our attention to appears to be endless and is presented as urgent. The danger that is inherent in embracing an entertaining flavor is that the passion of an issue will be inflated at the expense of general understanding, which leads to the distortion of the broadcast agenda. Emotional issues can escalate, while less dramatic but equally serious issues are ignored and forgotten. It can be difficult to determine what topics are important to us and exhausting to pay attention to all of it. The mediascape screams for us to look at it, and we are convinced it is irresponsible for us to look away, even once. Even for experts and professionals, getting information can be overwhelming. If people don't figure out what is important to them and manage their own emotions, they can overreact, or worse, disengage. After all, who of us wants to read the encyclopedia of barely pronounceable ingredients on a candy bar wrapper before we just decide to eat it anyway?

An enlightened citizenry is made free to exercise responsible self-governance, but it faces challenges from the tsunami of information that is contributed by a nearly infinite number of real and questionable sources.

Regulatory pressure exists, but it can be circumvented by loopholes, creative language, and unethical parties. If technology brings contentment to us from anywhere in the world, we are each of us vulnerable to interpretation and suggestive influences. Achieving a general understanding of the news is more difficult than ever. Journalists and media outlets who are financed by benefactors with ambitions and agendas are driven to present the facts through an obscured lens. The ethical standards the public tends to attribute to journalists can fall prey to sloganeering such as "truth to power" and "democracy dies in darkness." Until news stories are presented in an accessible way that clarifies fact versus opinion, identifying bias, disinformation, opinion, and rumor and distinguishing these from truth, objectivity, and facts is something we must do for ourselves. A way to do this effectively might be to discuss the news, share stories from our communities in a fair and responsible way, and engage in honest and topically relevant debates.

We think that a healthy citizenry and a responsible population should have the confidence to discuss current events and matters of interest in an open-minded way. Adults and children alike are constantly absorbing the news at home, via overheard conversations, and even from playground gossip. Just as it is up to us to determine what is healthy and desirable before we put it in our shopping carts, it is up to us to fact-check together, to learn how to identify trustworthy sources of news, and to encourage discussions about what is going on in the world as we eat dinner together, ride together on the bus, or wait in line to buy our groceries.

VI
We Get by with a Little Help from Our Friends

*People are always in good company
when they are doing what they really enjoy.*

—Samuel Butler

Whether we feel like shopping with friends or shopping solo, whether we do it out of necessity or just for fun, we try to enjoy shopping whenever we can. When it comes to picking out the perfect sleeping bag or getting a quality electric drill, we got that covered. When it comes to getting a pair of glasses that look good or clothes that don't make us look like we're stuck in the 1990s, we need a second opinion. Being adventurous can make even the most mundane shopping enthralling, even if you're just getting new shoes. Some of us would rather browse mindlessly in a home improvement store or a camping supply outfitter than spend ten minutes shopping for clothes or fight the slow-moving crowds in an oversized supermarket. It helps us if we know what tempts us to spend money, what we hate doing, when to shop alone, and when to shop with friends.

Sometimes shopping alone can be wise, but most stores and shops are created to bring people together in ways that other places don't. You shouldn't feel odd for wanting to get your shopping done by yourself if that's what you feel like doing. If you happen to be short on time, this is the way to go; the solo shopping experience is almost always quicker because most of us are influenced by what others think and do.

When we have an audience, we may shop differently. Social pressures and shows of economic prowess may lead us to buy more expensive things or more items than we want and browse through things and in places that we have no interest in. Shopping alone allows you the chance to take your time and shop at your own pace, without anyone complaining because you want to look through the book section instead of the antique furniture department.

The retail industry is expertly skilled at making us buy something that costs twice as much, like a fancier dress, a faster car, or a bigger house than we would prefer to buy. The pressures to spend money and acquire things comes from our peers, the store itself, and our own temptations. These pressures can be a lot to handle at once. When we make purchases that we don't really benefit from, we walk out of the store with less money and can look forward to buyer's remorse.

When we go shopping with others, it usually becomes an event that includes eating out, catching a movie, or hitting up multiple stores that everyone in the group is interested in. Events like this can greatly increase what we end up spending, both in time and money. Some, if not most, people are careful about not looking like they don't know how to, or are unable to, have fun. Being frugal around others makes some people self-conscious, and they may worry about looking cheap, uptight, or tasteless. It can have the opposite effect as well: spending what we want around economically minded people and those with tighter budgets can lead to shoppers being made to feel wasteful and extravagant.

Shopping alone frees shoppers of others' opinions, impressions, and buyers' remorse. Going out with friends might be more fun; just be mindful of the extra cost. When you are by yourself, it means no interruptions or distractions. Time alone, getting used to your intentional spending choices, can help solidify your determination and contentment so you're less susceptible to temptations and manufacturers' pressures. Shopping alone can help to achieve financial goals with greater efficiency and happiness.

When we're undecided about whether or not to buy something that we don't need, we put it down and decide to wait to get it another time. If we end up deciding that we want it, we can go back and buy it after we've given it some thought. Chances are we're happy with the extra time we used to make the decision, and we end up getting something we'll enjoy for a long time. There are always times we enjoy having friends or a loved one with us to bounce ideas off of, especially if we're unsure about a certain style or quality.

NO STRINGS ATTACHED

Not all shopping buddies are created equally. There will be those in our social circle who have different tastes and values than we do; some have differing judgments of what a worthwhile purchase is, while others are shopaholics themselves who love spending money, no matter what it's for. Instead of shopping with those people, we usually make the trip with those who'll give us their honest opinions and don't pressure us into buying things that we won't need or want. There's no use spending any amount of money on something if we'll never use, appreciate, or see it (because it's stuffed somewhere in the back of the top shelf).

Even the most independent of us needs company now and then. While you might think that you want to go alone, it could turn out that it would have been better with a friend as that way you wouldn't have had to second-guess your purchases by yourself. Need advice? Unsure what color brings out your eyes? Wonder which eyeglasses frame your face best? Go shopping with a friend who knows you well enough to know what suits you and your lifestyle. Your family and friends are there to be truthful about what's a good fit but even more importantly, what isn't. Another good tip what you could follow before you start your shopping adventure is to tell those whom you take with you what it is you're looking to buy. In this way, you set yourself a goal and commit to something. Commitment has been shown by research to be a very effective way of getting the things done that you want to get done without departing from your set goal. Plus, you are less likely in this scenario to be bombarded with lots of different things to look at that you don't want or need.

Good company will let you take your time going back and forth about something and point out when you over-analyze a purchase. Bringing a friend, brother, or niece who wants to join you can turn any shopping venture into more than just another errand, and it may become a bonding experience, worthwhile social investment, and source of some fun memories.

* * *

When we seek to learn about the world's events, either out of necessity or just to pass the time, we try to find the truth behind whatever is being conveyed. Whether it's by reading articles, scanning reports, or watching news broadcasts, we seek to understand the context of what transpires in the world, and sometimes that context is bigger than what our knowledge can grasp. It can usually be enough for us to soak in current events on our own, but often it helps us to find a truer, or larger, context by discussing what we have heard in the news with others.

Politics includes any interest that goes beyond personal interactions. Politics surrounds all of us and is the concern of every person on our planet. In democratic societies you vote for those politicians that are supposed to stand in for your country's well-being while considering the well-being of the world you live in. Of course, many people have their own opinions, and these might align with yours or not. So, hearing about what's going on in the world and considering everything in a political context can be a delicate way to bond with others—or become a surefire way to end a relationship. It can be burdensome but worth it to take into consideration the perspectives of other people.

Human beings are the one species that has the advantage of being able to empathize with others—whether the other is a fellow human or a living being from another species. But we also must remind ourselves that we see and experience the world from our own eyes with our own way of processing information. The way we interpret information might not always be the best way. Therefore, it's beneficial to discuss politics with others, especially with those who have a different opinion. This helps to broaden our horizons so we might learn about points of view of other people that we've never considered before. We might even change our minds and change for the better. The more consequential a view someone holds about a policy, politician, or event, the more important it is to know when and how to invite others to discuss certain news stories. Making friends with someone means paying attention to what you have in common with them, as well as what you don't. You might enjoy their sense of humor, their kindness, their taste in music, or their willingness to help you out in a pinch. It also helps to understand their principles, their social perspectives, their political views, and how curious and flexible they can be around new information. To avoid conflict, it helps to know these qualities about your friends and loved ones before you lambaste a governmental policy or feed one side of a topical controversy. This doesn't mean we can't or shouldn't invite political discourse into our relationships. It only means that we should perhaps take the time to learn how to dance, so to speak, so that we don't bump awkwardly into the other dancers on the floor.

A friend or loved one who is honest when interpreting the news and does their best to stop you from believing some of the misinformation you might read or hear is a treasure and should be appreciated. The key here is to be open to a different opinion and to even be open to change your own. A well-informed person can be like a dance partner. They don't have to walk in your footsteps to dance well with you, and with enough skill anyone can dance well to the music. Just because they hold different principles or opinions doesn't mean you have to fight. If someone asks during a political conversation when you first started believing certain ideas or where you heard something you told them, it can be easy for us to get defensive and argumentative. If someone asks us to reconsider certain issues, and if they remind us to consider multiple sources, we know that it isn't to challenge our values or attack us personally (usually) but rather because doing so services the integrity of our conversation and friendship.

Some of the most meaningful conversations with family and friends helped both of us, personally, to change our minds on issues we thought we had all figured out, and they've only broadened our understanding of how global events affect people and have maybe even allowed us to get to know our loved ones better. Getting past our own egos and biases isn't easy for any of us, but it is necessary if we'd rather be a wise person than a closed-minded person. After decades of accepting the limitations of our own perspectives, we benefit by continuing to challenge our own viewpoints and beliefs. We benefit from consulting regularly with people who see things in a different way. Being politically literate means that we can't simply avoid exchanging political opinions just because we know someone won't agree with us.

Political conversations between friends shouldn't be about who is right and who is wrong, although we often act as if they are. It's not fun to hold a conversation with a person whose beliefs are immovable or who is unwilling to change in the presence of new information. Exploring political points with an open-minded and curious person is an opportunity to discover the truths of humanity and even come up with new solutions to certain problems. Depending on the people you speak with about current events, you may want to approach certain topics with tact and sensitivity rather than raw judgment and harsh opinions, even if you feel justified in doing so. Not everyone is ready to hear that they don't need to buy ten pairs of skinny jeans, just as not everyone is ready to listen to criticisms of their cultural leaders' decisions. Political viewpoints, like the things we spend our money on, can be deeply connected to our sense of identity. If you get so focused on persuading at the expense of discussing, a person will withdraw from the conversation and digest news and events on their own rather than feel comfortable in the exchange of ideas. Instead of trying to change someone's mind about a biased news source or a certain political topic, it might be more productive if everyone tries to relax, check their egos, and enjoy the discussion.

Our brains crave novelty and learning. If we can move beyond the ego and regularly question the things that we assume we know, we can improve our discourse, and as a result, our political awareness will be more truthful. An ability to adapt with each information exchange is healthy for our minds and may even help us live longer lives.

Whenever we lose track of time and are pressured to buy things that we don't want or need, then we need to take a break so we can reorient ourselves and remember what is important. It can be just as easy to get disoriented and heated during a conversation that tackles issues near and dear to us. Knowing when to take a break, pause for a drink, or even walk away from that topic can save a friendship and allow time for stubborn minds to warm up to new ideas. When a conversation doesn't benefit those who are in it, is no longer fun, or is becoming more about winning and losing than exchanging ideas and discovering truth, it deserves a break. A strong relationship with loved ones and friends is infinitely more important than whatever political differences might develop.

Most people want the same things: personal safety, economic prosperity, good health, and social stability. Our political perspectives are simply different expressions of this. If avoiding politics or current events is damaging your relationship, try to simply have a respectful conversation about nonpolitical principles, just to start. Try to listen with an open mind and remember that you're likely to learn something new if you're able to keep your own opinions in check. If the other person expresses an interest in learning more about your own point of view, don't try to persuade them. Share your thoughts in a way that shows you've been listening to what they've said. If your friend respects a policy that you don't like, genuinely try to find things about the policy that you can empathize with and respect. When you attribute (or misattribute) negative motives to things your friend likes without being able to articulate a logical reason, you'll damage your friendship. Simply telling someone that they have an ugly house doesn't help. It is tolerable, and even appreciated, if you speak mindfully about their décor, location, furniture arrangement, etcetera. Even if there is very little you like about a new perspective, there will usually be something that you probably haven't thought of, and you might find that you like it. Seeking out identifiable points in an opposing political perspective to maintain, or even build, a relationship is a noble effort. In the end, you might both learn something from the other's point of view and even meet somewhere halfway, where you agree that no one was right.

Perhaps most importantly, we must be open to disagreeing without hard feelings. If keeping up decent conversation with people of opposing viewpoints were easy, everyone would do it. What often threatens to tear people apart isn't the mere misinterpretation of the news but rather the deliberate weaponization of it through the use of certain conflicting terms. Such antagonism, especially when modeled by cultural leaders and by media commentators, echoes on in political discussions, even between friends and family. Differing viewpoints frequently lead to heated posturing and an aggressive manner that influences our behaviors long after the discussion has been had. How we argue, and how our friends and loved ones argue with us, about our views of world events usually affects how and whether we participate in political processes. When others know how we contribute to world politics, like how we voted, if we contributed to some campaign, or the principles we champion, they might challenge our standing in our social groups, which directly affects our sense of security. Yet there are those who simply just don't care about politics, and if you try to call them to action, it will be met by a reaction that can be misinterpreted as general apathy or a lack of caring.

It is upon us to not become disengaged or avoid discussing those things we hold most dear and to communicate effectively and with tact so that our ideas are not bounded by impenetrable walls. Any fixed system of beliefs that allows for no additional information to enter is a delusional system. When people are willing to learn from each other, work together to broaden their understandings of issues, and choose their words wisely, such discussions lead to better ideas that progress our wellbeing and serve to deepen relationships. Certain terms carry an almost unmatched power simply because they cut to the quick of whatever surrounds the issues being discussed.

Few words used in the field of current events are wielded as aggressively as "nationalism" and "patriotism." These two concepts are viewed, at first, to be noble and admirable. In conjunction with current events and political summaries, however, calling people unpatriotic or nationalistic can affect how we interpret the actions of others relative to our continued cultural prosperity and our sense of safety. When our safety is threatened, we tend to make hasty decisions without consulting more effective alternatives or verifying the source. Most people see a patriot as someone who is respected and revered for putting the interests of their country ahead of their own distractions and goals. The word conjures an image of hardworking, unselfish citizens that we might even imagine as cultural icons. Patriots answer the call to help society in times of need and do the right thing. Nationalists are passionately invested in their own country ahead of others and sometimes even at the expense of them. Their ideas culminate in a sense of national identity that suggests a strong "us versus them" perspective. The term "nationalism" evokes extremist, sometimes illegal, tendencies that are associated with narrow-mindedness and imagined supremacy. Nationalists see themselves as willing to go above and beyond the system to defend the country, even if it means committing horrendous crimes.

Sometimes the line is blurred between patriots and nationalists. The dominant class uses the misinterpretation of these powerful concepts to serve its interests by galvanizing people and fomenting discord through argument and accusation. Government leaders use aggressive rhetoric deliberately to garner public support for war and other would-be-controversial decisions they make. Citizens are regularly led to support policies that are against global, national, and local interests in the name of "patriotic duty." Loyalty is a concept vital to the nationalist message because it is easy to impart, especially if it is presented as helpful to a volunteer service, like a nation's military. Activists who circumvent nationalist rhetoric are historically disenfranchised by those who wield hegemonic power. Those who rebel against the nationalistic message are looked down upon by the general public simply because it is all too easy to make them seem disloyal to patriotic ideals. Even if these hardworking and open-minded souls speak to nobler goals than those of the establishment, the way words are loaded and weaponized can turn people against each other more effectively than almost anything else.

It can help us, as individuals and as cultures, to accept that we might not have everything figured out and we will not agree on everything. Even if they are with friends and family who are on the same page as us, political conversations can still raise anxieties if we aren't sufficiently open-minded and mindful of the words we say. Sometimes something as simple as individual sense of security can lead to higher discourse and enlightened political thinking. Acknowledging the role of safety in a person's philosophy might help you have a fulfilling political exchange with those who disagree.

When we are facing the world together side by side, we can talk about almost anything, no matter if we agree or disagree, without feeling unrecognized or risking our sense of safety. Growing together is much more secure than working against each other. From a position of safety, acknowledgment, and shared understanding, we can take it when our ideologies clash with our those of our friends who insist that we have shitty taste in fashion and tell us we shouldn't go clothes shopping by ourselves.

Sometimes our friends aren't wrong.

VII
Make a Good Argument

Don't raise your voice, improve your argument.

—Desmond Tutu

As shoppers, many of us base our buying decisions not only on our personal needs but also often on our emotions. We human beings are ruled by emotions. Over 90 percent of our daily decisions are made by the experiential and emotional brain (system 1 thinking).[1] Even those of us who are stone-cold and in complete control of our reactions and expressions are led by our emotional impulses, especially when we think we are in control. Part of the joy we feel when we are having fun shopping, whether it's for clothes, tools, cars, or airplane tickets, comes from the emotional highs we get from spending money. That moment we get to take possession of something new and interesting, especially if it is something we have been coveting or waiting to get for a long

---

1. REF for system 1 / system 2 thinking.

time, is filled with a kind of blissful triumph that transcends logic and reason. Moreover, once we possess it, we value it unreasonably more than before we possessed it. Suddenly, we are no longer willing to part with things for the same price we spent.[1] No matter if we are among others or by ourselves, we are capable of monstrously unwise decisions that sometimes lead to certain regret if we succumb to our ungoverned feelings.

Most of us have probably noticed that managing our emotions is different from suppressing them. Ignoring the glee that comes with imagining that we live in a better house or pretending we don't desire a higher-quality pair of jeans won't make those emotions go away. Smarter purchasing decisions begin with acknowledging our feelings while also recognizing that they don't have to be in control. If we don't pay attention to our feelings as we consider what we buy, our actions can often end up being irrational and difficult to explain. Case in point: when someone likes to get a specific brand of perfume because they are subliminally reminded of their mother, who used to wear a similar-smelling perfume, by it, this is emotionally based decision-making. Someone who only likes to get a specific brand of whiskey because it's their brother's favorite sees it as a way of staying close to him, even if they are miles apart. Others develop a die-hard loyalty toward certain brands or products because they have a deep appreciation for or emotional attachment to it and want to support it, even if it is more expensive than comparable alternatives.

1. REF for endowment effect.

When people camp overnight at a store when a new product is about to be released, it's out of brand loyalty, not necessity. An emotional loyalist will be unlikely to switch from their chosen brands, no matter how good the competitor's newest offerings are. Loyal customers dedicate themselves not only to brands or products but also to shops and stores. Loyal shoppers can make up less than 20 percent of a customer base but make up more than 50 percent of base sales. Cultivating a stable core of repeat customers is a primary goal of business, and it's no different for shops. When people become emotionally invested in a certain product, manufacturer, or retailer, they become a valuable and effective voice for the seller across institutions, generations, and social circles. Special offers, reward programs, and exclusive content can be easy ways for retailers to fuel new interest as well as customer loyalty, establishing levels of trust and emotional attachments that all but guarantee future business transactions.

Any good business knows that the key to earning future visits and larger transactions from you, not to mention getting you to recommend it to your family members and friends, goes beyond low prices. Even though prices matter, they are far less important than is assumed in traditional economics theory. After all, if a product is priced lower than at other places but is of insufficient quality, it won't be seen as a worthwhile purchase. More importantly, even if the quality is the same, branding makes customers perceive the product as of higher quality and therefore influences them to spend more on that product of equal quality.

A good business earns repeat visits by offering quality merchandise at a price you like, as well as an array of services that make the shopper trust that they are making the right decisions to spend money there. Let's say that we want to buy a new computer because the one we had got ran over by an ex-girlfriend. When we go shopping for a new computer, we don't just want to get a computer we want for a price we feel is reasonable, but we also want the option to return it if it is defective out of the box. If a store we're already fond of has a sale on computers, we'll start shopping at that store first. If we end up getting a replacement computer, it means that the store, the computer brand, and the product itself have all made winning arguments for their purchase and we agreed with them. It may as well mean that because of our brand loyalty to our favorite store, we're convinced to buy that specific computer there and not elsewhere. If we decide to keep the computer until it gets run over by someone else, we'll probably go to the same store and see if we can get that same brand and product because we feel like we can trust these businesses and their wares.

No lasting relationship ever made a convincing argument without the element of trust. Places of commerce can be different in countless ways, but two ways they are all the same are the fact that they want to impart a pleasant emotional experience to their customers and cultivate a bond of trust with their customers. One way to do this is to lead people to understand the value of products and services available. How shopkeepers decide to deal with concerns and problems is what instills trust and loyalty. Retailers help to instill trust in the buying process by establishing return policies for their products, inviting shoppers to apply for reward programs, and many other policies that make customers feel that the retailer cares about them—or about their continuing business, at least. There is more than trust-building to those offers. They work like a hook for customers. Once we are part of the brand loyalty program and accumulate more points, we go back to the same store to get even more points. Return policies are a neat trick that makes use of several psychological phenomena, two of which stand out: regret aversion and the endowment effect. People often fear the regret of having made a bad decision, but once you know you can return the product, it takes away this fear at an instant. People value something more once they possess it, and we will probably fear the loss of not having this product, and this might become more painful for us than returning it and receiving a refund is pleasurable for us. Of course, that's only true if the product serves our purpose. We are happy to return it and receive a refund if the product is a total failure. Unfortunately, we all too often only realize this after the refund policy has expired.

At each step of the transaction, shopkeepers and retailers can easily damage or work to enhance the emotional bond between their customers and their place of business. Professionals know that they must be honest with their employees and customers, and if they get caught in a lie, no one will trust them. Trust is only ever built over time. A way that many shopping places establish trust is by surprising and delighting clients and customers. Sellers know that to outsell their competitors, they must strive to deliver more services, more conveniences, and more awareness of their clients' demands. Delivering more than customers expect goes a long way toward building trust, which is a surefire way to speak to customer emotions. And emotions, more than almost anything else, govern us as customers and as human beings.

Trustful interaction serves the interests of those involved. Trust itself may be analyzed as an emotion and is, therefore, independent of rational deliberation to some extent. Trust enables us to cope with risk. If we want to promote trustful interaction, especially when we are exchanging hard-earned money and time for uncertain products and services, we must depend upon shared values and develop emotions that lead us toward trust. We don't want to shop on *their* terms. We're better off shopping on *our* terms!

* * *

Discussions, especially political discussions, usually operate on some level of trust and almost always involve some emotional context. When we are talking about things that matter, our passions rise to the surface, and a sense of trust is key to making even the most controversial topics navigable. We can probably all understand from experience that when people deliberately distort words or intentions, it betrays the spirit of communication itself. It becomes propaganda, falsely assigns values, goals, and positions to people, misrepresents the argument, and takes away the integrity of discourse. This kind of lying can be found in media broadcasts and news articles and is legally permitted in opinion pieces that look so much like harmless informational sources. We might think we are immune to the siren call of media sources that appeal to our political leanings, and we would be galactically incorrect.

We all have principles, preferred social ideals, and some of us have even cultivated an articulated political ideology. People who adhere firmly to a political idea, party, faction, or cause are partisan, and they tend to exhibit an allegiance to their personal politics. This can be a good thing, as has been expressed by some philosophers. Political economist John Stuart Mill wrote in *On Liberty* that "a party of order or stability, and a party of progress or reform, are both necessary elements of a healthy state of political life." In addition, economist Graham Wallas said that "something is required simpler and more permanent, something which can be loved and trusted, and which can be recognized at successive elections as being the same thing that was loved and trusted before; and a party is such a thing." These points highlight what is so appealing about political parties: they give people who subscribe to them a sense of trust and positive emotional experiences. Safety and trust mean much to people, especially when there is so much distrust and uncertainty in political discourse.

When there's no trust, it makes it difficult for us to talk about politics with people and still stay friends with them. If we can't talk politics without hurt feelings or seeing the other side of an issue, then we need to become better communicators. It is possible to maintain inner peace, especially if we remind ourselves as we begin a political discussion that we're not right about everything. No one is. Dedication to what is right can be seen as noble and worthwhile, but refusing to look beyond a rigid ideology makes meaningful communication difficult.

Communicating better means forming constructive arguments so that we can succeed in sharing knowledge and perspectives, as opposed to imposing our principles or ideologies on others. When people misattribute negative motives and beliefs to people who disagree with them or to other political parties, it is a small step to derogatory labeling trivializing the points and intentions of others. Refusing to acknowledge people's values ends conversations, sours arguments, and hurts relationships. Although we aren't automatically given to constructively arguing, it upholds the integrity of communication if we all try hard to listen to an opposing perspective. When we discuss politics with friends and loved ones, we can maintain, or even deepen, our healthy relationships if we make it a habit to treat what others say respectfully and make an honest effort to see differing perspectives in the best possible light. Understanding other concerns allows us to focus on the information that makes a constructive argument, especially if we submit our own thoughts and ideals without diminishing others'. The commonly held view of arguments is that they lead to problems in our personal and social lives—and that misses the point of arguing in the first place.

We think the most productive arguments take place between those who wish to learn, not to win. Before inviting people to argue, we like to take just a second to crystallize in our minds what it is that we're about to argue for and what it is we ultimately want. Do we want the other person to just understand our point of view? Are we seeking to accomplish a specific goal? If it's not a realistic or obtainable goal, a discussion that can wander into toxic territory can result. This is not only a surefire way for us to keep others from sharing our perspectives but will also likely damage a relationship. Some healthy responses within an argument include challenging the facts the other person is using, challenging the conclusions they draw from those facts, and accepting the points they are making but arguing for the significance of other relevant points and showing that one idea reasonably follows another. Use logic as well as emotion by appealing to worthy motives that are hard to disagree with. While our politics may be wildly different, our principles often overlap.

Bringing an open mind to arguments benefits all of us, and after making the effort, we are able to better understand opposing points of view. Putting aside ego and emotions allow us to develop more accurate beliefs, more reliable awareness of the facts, and deeper understanding of the issues. We cannot learn from any arguments if we can't trust others to express their real values. Constructive conversation becomes difficult when people forget to appreciate each other and work together. Even the smallest amount of disrespect or aggression can make people feel that their identity is being threatened, which can quickly make them closed-minded. It's safe to say that people are much more likely to remain open-minded when they argue gently and kindly rather than aggressively. It helps to affirm our respect for whomever we're arguing with, even if we're telling them some hard truths.

To endear even the most hard-headed arguers to our points, we must do the research that underlies the arguments we uphold, and that is some difficult, heavy lifting. Most people don't go the distance to verify the reliability and authenticity of their arguments. A frighteningly enormous amount of the media-consuming population avoids doing their own research before forming opinions. A responsible citizen does the reading before wielding opinions carelessly in their discussions and in their political decisions. You must talk to any competent person you can find and listen to their arguments. It takes overcoming the ego to listen and chase down arguments that run counter to our established views, but until we learn to see issues through multiple lenses, we might, at any time, be fooling ourselves.

Mastering our emotions is key to keeping our emotions from controlling us. Becoming our own harshest critics means that sometimes we must have the intellectual honesty to occasionally reexamine some of our most deeply cherished political ideas. Our innate desire to seek out only information that confirms what we believe we know is powerful, but we can demand better of ourselves than our base instincts by cultivating disciplined minds and compassionate hearts. In any conversation and whenever we seek new information, we all should be aware of confirmation bias—the tendency to look for information that confirms our currently held beliefs, that confirms the information we already have.

DR. CHRIS HOMAN AND THOMAS DUDEK

In high school debate class, students are tasked with forming an argument about a particular issue, then without preparation asked to defend the opposing debate points. Considering the arguments on the other side of any issue is the key to responsible information gathering. To have an opinion while being able to state the arguments for the other side is necessary for us as people to work *with* the world rather than against it. By doing the heavy lifting of learning, researching, communicating truthfully, and rising above our egos, we are capable of respecting the entire argument, both sides. When we do not make these efforts, we are not arguing on our terms but on someone else's terms. Those are most likely the terms we have been instilled with during our childhood and youth. But now, as adults, we must acknowledge and seize the power that we have been given. Only by taking stock of our emotions can we speak intelligently about our politics. Just as shoppers prefer to spend their money and time at places and with retailers they trust, responsible citizens will entertain ideas and political values if the sources make their arguments in a trustworthy way.

VIII
Politics and Piracy

Education without values, as useful as it is, seems rather to make man a more clever devil.

—C. S. Lewis

Pirates have been around for centuries. As long as the ocean has carried ships carrying valued goods, there have been those willing to take them over. Getting things the easy way is the essence of piracy, and it has kept us in awe because although pirates usually didn't live very long, pleasure was their only real desire. The romanticizing of pirates in literature and popular culture has led some of us to think they were just swashbucklers living a life of pleasure on the seas, fighting only if they had to. Pirates preferred to take their treasures without a fight, but when they fought, they were ruthless. They realized that it was effective to incite fear by taking prisoners and keeping their belongings. Although pirates were depicted as aggressive and uncivilized people, their earnings justified their way of life, turning many of them into the wealthier members of society, even though they were, in fact, criminals.

In the realm of commerce, there are many treasures. A person's time, attention, and opinion are often just as lucrative to certain agencies as what customers spend. If a profitable transaction is a gold coin, then a loyal customer is worth more than buried treasure. Good customer experiences depend on the confidence and trust the customer has in the seller. If the seller distorts the truth, even a little bit, the buyer has a way to respond to unethical marketing. If companies abuse the customer, they just might find themselves in a public relations debacle, all because they didn't satisfy the moral or ethical standards of their customers.

Aristotle took the word *ethical* to mean those qualities we think of as spiritual, such as moderation, courage, and generosity. Morals affect the social conscience and influence people's behavior. Morals typically are part of a bigger system of social norms, which are principles of how to live one's life, the dos and don'ts of living within a given social system. These principles of right and wrong suggest a general model of behavior to guide us as individuals and as a collective. Our agreed-upon ethical standards promote certain values, like honesty, justice, equality, impartiality, kindness, and freedom (to name just a few) as certain norms we can all strive toward.

Well, *most* of us.

Those of us looking for a more dependable way to acquire our possessions than resorting to piracy can buy things in a way that satisfies not only our needs and wants but also the needs and wants of society at large.

One way to focus on the collective good, just in terms of how we choose to fill our shopping carts, is to try to get products that are sourced in a responsible and sustainable way relative to social causes we cherish and in ways we understand to hurt the environment less than others. As we become more eco-conscious customers, we learn more about what our purchases mean for the planet and the people producing them. As a result of the growing public attention to production methods, companies find that when they commit to ethical and moral business practices, it benefits both consumers and businesses. Ethical sourcing that focuses on human rights, environmental impact, and social impact is about truth and transparency.

Customers are likely to boycott a brand and refuse to purchase from a company that betrays their ethics, and smart companies are paying attention. This is called *identity economics*. People identify with certain values and moralities, and companies who realize this can fare much better than those who don't. Some companies may even outcompete their competitors who weren't willing to change their business model, solely focusing on costs, profits, and efficiency. While many retailers learn about ethical sourcing practices because they want to mitigate risks, reduce operating costs, protect their brand image, and meet consumer demand to increase sales, the results lead to massive wins. Providing the consumer peace of mind and a feeling that they are helping make their world a better place by their shopping decisions isn't just good ethics; it's good business.

Stores, sellers, and manufacturers that ignore social pressures and persist in unethical sourcing are vulnerable to being cruel, destructive, and immoral. Even unethical decisions made along the supply chain leading to the customer, no matter how removed from the public eye, might be discovered in time. Ethical approaches start with behaving transparently, inviting shoppers to provide feedback, engaging more directly and knowingly with the supply base, and taking small, manageable steps toward ethical sourcing. Ignoring the public might make companies seem like modern-day pirates who are only interested in getting what they haven't earned, even if it is only the trust of their customers. Transparency is key to a trusted reputation. As shoppers, we have the responsibility and ability to bend even the most powerful retailers to our ethical will. Voting with our business, time, and money adds up significantly over weeks, years, and generations.

* * *

The places and people that we receive news from are almost as important as the news itself. As academics tell us, the source of information tells us how reliable the information is and whether we can trust the facts contained within. Just as retailers can acquire their merchandise through channels and methods that vary from ethical to horrendous, powerful agencies have been known throughout history to control information through behaviors that are direct, aversive—even by using physical force or threats of force. We try to pay attention to reporters and news agencies that avoid using information to manipulate; rather, we like to think that we get information from agencies that circulate the news with a spirit of reciprocity, cooperation, unsolicited help, and compassion. When we see the news being broadcast in a way that employs coercive strategies without consideration for the goals or motivations of the social environment at large, we take care with how much trust we give to them. Even if the source is distrustful and overly casual with his or her opinion sharing, we might continue to listen because it can be just as relevant to know the misinformation going around as to know the verifiable data backed up by evidence. We try to stay informed through media sources who share the kind of holistic, cooperative outlook that we work to maintain. If we see that media outlets present current events through a lens that perpetuates zero-sum thinking, and we do, we should watch with skepticism. After all, there *are* pirates, lots of them, who benefit by putting out misinformation and calling it news.

When pirates get control of information, it is upon us, you and me, to manage our trust in reported information ourselves and know when what we are told is real and when what is being constructed by those with agendas is a fictional narrative. We are aware of how music, presentation, and perceived presence of authority gives anything we are told a sense of gravitas, especially when it plays with our dopamine levels. Ordinary citizens can't do much about how information is presented to us, but we can defend against misinformation by arming ourselves against those who would mislead us, just as conscientious shoppers choose where they make their purchases. Arming ourselves means keeping an eye out for agendas that are being promoted.

The presentation of misinformation in certain political states has been closely tied to authoritarian powers and heavily promotes nationalism and corporate power, as well as industrial and military might, as the best solutions to economic woes. One should take care when seemingly harmless media outlets promote the superiority of the nation. Such a relationship between an upper class and its journalistic sources can become antidemocratic because it devalues electoral, parliamentary, and multiparty systems, which frustrates the goal of national greatness. Similarly, immigration, which has always been a topic of fear and controversy at the best of times, engenders widespread national resentment when presented by news reporters with an opinionated spin. Factual economic reports especially can be made to generate disbelief and anger among people who are emotionally bonded to their untruths.

A combination of national resentment, manipulated information, and misplaced public trust allows abusive powers to rise, even in the most democratic of countries. Misinformed minds and narrowly focused nostalgia can combine to aggravate anger stemming from socioeconomic inequalities caused by upper class–controlled systems. As hostilities toward "the other" increase, the lines of cultural inclusion and exclusion among the population are subtly redrawn by information manipulators. When a segment of the population is gradually vilified by those who are respectable journalists, people become less united and citizens can be made to fight against citizens instead of uniting together against the real oppressor. Political participation is often demanding for citizens, so when ordinary people are manipulated and misinformed, they become less likely to effect change or influence powerful institutions. In essence, the number of "democracy-capable" citizens is diminished when the public is no longer informed of the truth. Citizens, no matter how compassionate and well-meaning, can only fulfill their role and meet the requirements of democracy if they are politically literate. Without political literacy, the functionality and survival of a democracy is at stake.

There are those who are exhausted by the misdirection and lies they see reported, and these tired souls argue that to not vote at all is better than to vote. If voting means that a person condones the actions of the power who gets their vote, then is the voter not complicit in the actions they have voted in favor of? This kind of reasoning does not encourage people to participate in the system and can lead people to withdraw from public processes that they would likely improve simply by casting their vote. In a world where nothing ultimately matters, what role do ethics play?

Good and bad are human constructs, but they can be our compass in uncertain waters. Good and bad are important because they result in what we perceive to be long-lasting consequences. If the preservation of humanity and the betterment of society is the ultimate good, and that which leads to our despair and destruction is bad, we can begin to assign importance to ethical decisions in a universe that might seem indifferent. It is the person who sees their participation in the civic process as an opportunity to implement their own personal greater goods who helps society function more effectively.

It is worth emphasizing that political literacy is something most people find difficult in a world that is controlled by those who are all too eager for the general public to leave them alone to do what they want. So many of us are tempted to think that anything we might do of a political nature is in vain because we will all die one day, and none of it will matter. While this kind of thinking might be impossible to argue against, the philosophy runs counter to the needs of a society that relies on such fictions to maintain order. If we as citizens don't exercise our morality, nothing will stop the powers from committing acts of baseless cruelty.

Historically, when citizens garner enough attention to rally others against oppressive powers, media that is close to the state reports that such citizens are motivated by anarchists. Viewed as the ultimate "other," anarchists are typically painted as inherently dangerous. Thinking of anarchists as dangerous threats to social harmony is a vile misrepresentation, perpetuated repeatedly by those who wield power and can distort information. It helps to understand this by knowing that anarchism is a name given to a philosophy that suggests social harmony arises not by the submission to law or by obedience to any authority but by agreements made by the various groups that constitute it. Anarchism rejects compulsory rule and holds that society can be productive without a micromanaging, coercive state, especially if that state lacks moral legitimacy. Rather than violently rebel institutions, as most people are lead to imagine, most anarchist groups merely support a gradual change to free the individual from the oppressive laws and social constraints of the oppressive class-controlled state.

While there are several types of anarchism, they all agree that a free society must be sustained by free individuals. After all, the term traces back to the Greek word *anarkhia*, which means "without rulers" or "without authority." It stands for the absence of domination, hierarchy, and power over others. From this perspective, it can be imagined how a ruling class would paint those who protest their authority as rebels and deviants and even make them out to be as dangerous as terrorists. A mediascape that is firmly controlled by the upper class might easily turn citizen against citizen by manipulating information to its benefit and playing people against each other so they are too distracted to see the real threat at hand.

All media sources have the power to abuse the trust of their audiences, just as stores have the power to con shoppers into spending money on defective merchandise. It is up to us, as it has always been up to the citizenry, to become more politically literate. It pays to look up definitions of certain words that people, companies, politicians, and the news use. You may notice that in many cases these words are used in a different sense than the original meaning according to the dictionary. As we learn more about the politics around us, we must challenge the media when it strays from the truth and betrays our shared ethics and moral codes, lest we vote against our own interests and those of our loved ones.

IX
Knowing is Half the Battle

Ignorance more frequently begets confidence than does knowledge.

—Charles Darwin

Do you trust what you think you know?
Should you trust what you think you know?
Should *any* of us?

Most of us can appreciate how feeling a sense of confidence has helped us to move forward with new people and uncertain opportunities. When things didn't work out for us at first, as often happens, it was whatever confidence we could dig up that helped us to try the things we needed to again. Human minds are primed to try to make sense of the world, and it becomes only more difficult as we venture deeper into a disparate array of information as we try to glean information that can better inform our decisions. We sometimes fail to accurately judge our perspectives as we try to cut through the inundating confusion. As we work to interpret our own thoughts and abilities, we are affected by whatever sense of confidence and self-esteem we value in order to accomplish our goals. That confidence most of us work to nurture all our lives isn't innate; rather, it's gained through nothing less than experience and genuine work. Anything less simply results in hollow bluster and foolish fury.

Even those of us privy to information and honed by raw experience have areas where we are uninformed and uncertain. No one is an expert at everything. People can sometimes draw from their confidence in one area, mistakenly think that their intelligence and knowledge can extend into areas with which they are unfamiliar. When people fail to recognize this trait of overconfidence in themselves, they are more likely to engage in risk-taking behaviors, perhaps even foolhardy ventures. We don't mean to suggest that self-esteem and confidence are bad things. On the contrary, in the right amounts, these qualities can be of mighty service. As we have all heard in our tales of heroic folklore, confidence often leads to success, but in undue capacities, an inflated sense of confidence leads people to bluff their way through situations, often convincing others, even themselves, that they possess abilities they do not actually have. As we are all the center of our own worlds, it is often our perceptions, experiences, thoughts, needs, and wants that loom largest when we make decisions. Even at the best of times, unknown elements, when ignored, repressed, and unaccounted for, can manipulate us by inflating our sense of self and even our pride when we least expect it.

This kind of overconfidence, this cognitive bias, where people believe that they are smarter and more capable than they really are, is called the Dunning-Kruger effect. The term encapsulates the phenomenon of individuals, and even groups, being blind to their own ignorance. A combination of inadequate self-awareness and misplaced confidence leads people to overestimate their own capabilities. Overconfident people overestimate their own knowledge and abilities and are incapable of seeing their vulnerabilities. If it is not accompanied by modesty, this quality profoundly affects what people believe and the decisions they make. The knowledge a person needs to be good at something correlates with their ability to recognize when they are not good at something. For example, a person who has never ridden a horse might think that they are naturally good at it. It isn't until overconfident people actually sit in the saddle and go for a ride that they realize there is a lot more to it and they ought to show some respect to those who have mastered the skill. Until they try, overconfident people remain ignorant to their own inability.

Essentially, most people do not possess the skills needed to recognize their own limitations. You might be certain that this doesn't happen to you, that you are aware of yourself and your confidence is never played upon.

We have news for you. Even in places you have been shopping at since you were a child, if not *especially* in those places, you can be played. Don't you just love it when your local store has a loyalty program where you save money as you buy more things there? We, too, are led to think that we're wisely saving money, not to mention time, if we do all our shopping at the same place over and over again, but we would be foolish if we thought that the retailer itself wasn't actually the one making the profit off of our repeated business. Retailers have figured out that they can cut expenses by marketing toward existing customers rather than generating new business. There is profit in customer loyalty. While customers do get occasional bargains for being loyal to a certain store, retailers benefit from invaluable insight into customer spending trends. Sellers and marketers receive tracking data on your purchases without your ever knowing it. How much are people in your town or region spending on alcohol, sugar, tobacco, or firearms? Do you know?

Retailers do.

Retailers are experts at getting the data from your shopping habits, and the more you make purchases from each location or business, the more they know about how much you spent. They know what time you are likely to stop by, and they use the data to determine just how far they can bump up prices without persuading you to take your business elsewhere. While a classic buy-one-get-one-free offer might be a deal that we would feel silly passing up, such deals exist because supermarkets have hiked the price of the merchandise on sale. We would often be better off by ignoring what we think is a lucrative bargain in favor of looking for similar items that are more sensible purchases without the fanfare.

Marketers go beyond knowing your habits and behaviors; they can even predict what you are going to purchase in the future. Depending on your past shopping behaviors and slight, "sudden" changes in those, they know when you're about to move to a new house, when you're planning to have a child (or are pregnant), or when you change jobs. They see this because they have the data from millions of other customers who are like you, in similar life situations. From past behavior of other shoppers, marketers infer about your future behavior once you seem to make changes in your purchases. Marketers make use of their knowledge by marketing targeted products to which they know you will be much more susceptible or more likely to purchase in your current situation.

Stores play on our sense of value approximation by using comparative pricing to make consumers think they are getting a better deal than they are. By putting the average-priced item next to a more expensive organic item, retailers lead shoppers to conclude incorrectly that they will save money by choosing the cheaper item, when they're just paying the normal market price. The decoy-effect tactic is used to make you feel like you are getting a better deal than you are.

If you see prices ending with .90, .95, or .99, it is best to simply round the price up, and then you will get a better sense of the real price. Indeed, another tactic retailers use to play with our minds is the left-digit effect. This is a tool used by many retailers to distract shoppers, making them more likely to buy something that ends in .99 rather than a rounded amount because they tend to notice the number on the left when comparing price. We are wise to be aware of comparisons between products, especially if one of them seems to be a bad deal. If you see one product that you think is way overpriced, try to entirely disregard that option.

Where customers are encouraged to buy in bulk, they should take care that they aren't just being tricked into buying way more of a product than they intend. Sellers know that customers are willing to pay more for locally grown or sourced foods, which is why they display a picture of a friendly farmer near produce, hoping customers subliminally associate the goods with salt of the earth people. Stores deliberately price fruits and vegetables by weight knowing most shoppers aren't going to bother weighing each apple, tomato, or dragon fruit. We might just decide to get however many we want because our brains get tired after calculating figures and we experience decision fatigue. Even for people who are confident about their on-the-spot math skills, retail tactics play with peoples' confidence so that they feel that they got a good deal when they didn't.

As people learn more about a certain topic, they begin to simultaneously grasp a greater understanding of the topic while also recognizing their own lack of knowledge and ability. Confidence levels might dip at first when you confront your own ignorance about something you thought you had already mastered, but as you attain more information, your confidence levels start to rise once again. Rather than being from the hip troubleshooters, previously ignorant people become experts on a topic when they keep digging deeper. So can you!

To give our brains a rest so that we can draw from our experiences rather than be misled into thinking that we know more about what constitutes actual value than we do, we would be wise to put aside our egos and use a calculator to work out if those deals are really as cheap as they seem to be. There might be a part of us that thinks we should be able to do simple math in our heads when comparing prices, but we can still get lured, despite concerted efforts, into spontaneous spending increases because something appears to be an obvious bargain when it's not.

Not sure if you're confident or overconfident? It's a good idea to ask others that you trust and respect for a temperature check. Honest and constructive criticism can usually be difficult to hear, but it can ultimately provide valuable insights for us that we are unable to attain for ourselves. We might prefer to take this kind of medicine from people we love and enjoy over continuing to not know our own strengths and weaknesses. Even as others pass along valuable feedback, it can be all too easy to focus only on those things that confirm what you think you already know. This isn't narcissism or vanity, just a common type of psychological bias that experts call confirmation bias. To combat this self-defensive tendency, it is incumbent upon us to keep challenging our beliefs and expectations. We can only know for certain if we continually seek out information that challenges our perceptions. True value is obtained only when we realize that there is more to learn than what we already know. Until we overcome our hubris, we will continue to waste our time and keep spending more money than we ought to on things we don't really need or didn't even want in the first place (when we walked into the store).

* * *

If there are people who rush to assume that they are experts when they, in fact, do not know enough, then knowledgeable people, especially genuine experts, can trust their perceptions of their own facts and abilities, right?

Not always.

Not even *usually*.

The Dunning-Kruger effect suggests that people who are educated and competent tend to underestimate their own abilities compared to less knowledgeable people. This means that while experts, no matter the field or skill, know that they are better than average, they are more modest about themselves and possess less confidence than they should. The problem is that experts are inclined to judge everyone else to be as knowledgeable as they are. This is also called the curse of knowledge. Once you know, you assume others know too.

One of the single biggest reasons why more people do not engage in politics is because they're just not interested. In addition to the fact that there is a plethora of unreliable news sources, the growing awareness of the general public in the ubiquity of misinformation can dissuade many well-meaning souls from making their voices heard if so many feel that they don't know enough to bring anything worthwhile to the table. This has many consequences, but the most significant one is that those who think they know more than they do are likelier to participate in political conversations and impact real-world policies than those who judge themselves to be too unqualified. When a person votes, speaks to their local representative, or presses their opinions into a conversation, they affect the political machine.

Those who affect the political machine, even just by endorsing one representative or policy, know that doing so means they can be held somewhat responsible for whatever those representatives do or what effects those policies have. As informed citizens, we can see how politicians can lie and cheat without consequence far too often. Campaign promises are meaningless to those of us who pay attention to the political narratives because politicians are likely to say anything to gain supporters and can then act however they want once they attain power. From a certain perspective, knowledge breeds cynicism and erodes the faith in institutions that comes so easily to us when we are young and impressionable. When trust in people and systems is compromised, we begin to doubt what we think we know, and it is tempting to withdraw from those things that become unfamiliar.

Anytime we feel betrayed by some entity, be it a political representative or a supermarket, we learn to steer clear of it once and for all. Participating in any system, whether locally or on a grander scale, grants legitimacy to people, policies, or ideas that can only betray others the same way that we feel we have been betrayed. The idea of representatives of any political philosophy coercing others and impose their will on the general public is loathsome. For that reason, we can see how so many citizens view it to be immoral to participate in the political process. We tended to think that it was either hopeless for us to participate in the political process or that we didn't know enough of the world to make our voices heard. Even though we have traveled and lived in various countries, we still felt that we weren't as politically competent as others might be. Even if we wanted to comment on a policy or an event that political conversations centered on, we'd feel as though everyone would discover a lack of political awareness. We would try to watch and read more news to strengthen our grasp of politics, but instead of feeling more confident, we'd feel smaller in the face of all that we realized we did not know. As we engaged more with political news, it presented cognitive dissonances regarding the social infrastructures and cultural narratives we took for granted, loved, and supported.

The news is almost always negative and learning more about the culture in which we lived meant discovering deep flaws in the systems, deep flaws that we are beginning to see that we're helping to perpetuate, just by being a member of society. Learning more about political events can open the mind to uncertainty, and that can easily lead to us losing our footing. Morals are what push us to aspire toward the noblest ideals and principles. Acknowledging our lack of confidence in the face of a political environment so filled with misinformation, betrayal, and uncertainty shouldn't stop us from making our voices heard but can help us to become wiser citizens. Perhaps the very morality that people like us can bring to social systems is exactly what is needed for it to become more of what the general public expects and wants. Systems and institutions benefit when ordinary voices are heard. Voices like yours.

Our morals could be the foundation we need to recalibrate our perspectives and adjust to new facts, but we should take care to not become myopic and selfish about getting our causes attention. Other people have causes that are important as well and might even be more important than our own. We shouldn't think of ourselves as weak if we acknowledge others' causes to be more pressing than ours. If we can be open-minded about the importance of our values and allow that to reflect in our political views, why should we be deemed to be unqualified to exercise our rights as concerned and responsible citizens? If the only people who influence the political game are those who are confident and wildly misinformed, then we all end up suffering. We have choices to make, and each one of our choices influences the world, even in a small capacity.

Many citizens perceive the ramifications of even small political events as confusing. This can have the effect of making people feel like imposters, but political processes are endlessly complicated for even lifelong experts. It may be impossible to fully organize and comprehend the political world, but there's the rub, citizens! We can participate directly or indirectly. We *can* influence political decisions that might initially seem beyond us. Our ideologies extend from our ethics and are expressed by our thoughts about who we believe should make decisions, what moral principles should take precedence, and what policies decision makers should pursue.

There are almost endless reasons people might cite to justify why they don't vote, anything from anger at the government to concern that their participation holds them accountable to imagined political horrors. All topics, no matter their complexity, are accessible to those who take the time to understand the necessary fundamentals, attain a certain degree of humility, as well as maintain a willingness to learn. When a belief is directly challenged by new information, it is humility that allows us to process the new knowledge without feeling threatened. To overcome impostor syndrome, it helps to know what our core beliefs are and to acknowledge that being perfect so others approve of us is an illusion. We might think that there is some perfect image we must attain for us to be worthy of political conversations, and we would be mistaken.

To move past these feelings of academic and societal irrelevance, it is upon us to confront some of the most deeply ingrained beliefs that we hold about our ideas. This isn't just unpleasant or difficult, it's counterintuitive, especially when we are met with perspectives that seem ludicrous if we don't even realize that we hold certain biases. We can overcome our egotistic limitations by communicating effectively and sharing our feelings. With an open exchange of multiple ideas, we are likelier to identify irrational beliefs, even when they are deeply hidden and rarely examined. Confronting ourselves honestly and directly is almost as possible as eating an entire elephant. You know how to eat an entire elephant? One bite at a time. Don't take on too much at once; take baby steps instead. It is in our nature to either try to do things perfectly or decide they aren't worth doing at all. This can be as simple as offering an opinion or sharing a story about yourself when you're in a group conversation. If the conversation goes in a direction that makes you question your opinions and facts, you know things are getting interesting and the information exchange is worthwhile. When you reexamine your facts, take baby steps by simply looking at whether your thoughts are rational; don't try to solve an entire political issue at once.

Can you imagine how productive our conversations would be if we all focused on listening to what the other person is saying instead of preparing to attack and defend the principles being discussed? Rather than trying to automatically defend the perfection of our positions, being genuinely interested in learning more serves political discourse more effectively. Maintaining an illusion of perfection often goes together with imposter syndrome. It is exhausting when we set excessively high goals for ourselves, and when (not *if*, but *when*) we fail to maintain perfection, we can look forward to experiencing self-doubt and becoming defensive and closed-minded.

To move past this, it helps if we try looking at ourselves as works in progress, because that's what we are. Growth, in any sense, is a result of lifelong learning and skill-building. This applies to everyone, even the most confident people. It isn't smart to keep learning in life without letting ourselves grow from the experience. Realize there's no shame in asking for help when you need it. If you don't know how to do something, ask. If you can't figure out how to solve a problem, seek advice. Rather than feel bad for not knowing something you think you should, try to remember that there's always, *always* more for us to learn. There's nothing wrong with being confident, but if confidence comes from a narcissistic or abusive place, it risks damaging our political goals, our social relationships, and the cultural narratives we want to survive us.

As we have already discussed, when an honest political conversation, when we share our knowledge and feelings, we can better identify the biases and logical errors we harbor. Our flaws and vulnerabilities make us uncomfortable when we want to show our authority, but wise people accept that these flaws remind us that we are human. A fool who pretends to know as much as an expert is bound to ultimately fail and is likely up to no good. Such people don't spread wisdom; they are out to feed their egos or gain an illegitimate advantage by satisfying their closed-minded positions. These people have missed the point of political discourse and only wish to service short-term and hollow pursuits.

Maintaining integrity in our political discourse isn't a new or local idea; it is how cultures thrive and survive. In Greek mythology the goddess Memory, also named Clio, was viewed to be the mother of culture. Clio was revered as the torchbearer of history, which means that she was singularly responsible for keeping dependable accounts of human and natural events. She maintained an honest tale and told it repeatedly with unambiguous language that withstood the long passage of time. The reliable memory of past events in today's world still brings order to the indifference of chaos. Being a responsible citizen doesn't simply mean helping to influence the politics of our time but also acknowledging the needs and wants of the present. If well-meaning citizens defer to those with agendas to take control of the storytelling process, how big a role can truth play in the story of the human race?

Speaking truth to the memory of our time is the responsibility of all of us, and we are all qualified to do it. We shouldn't wait for the permission of those with agendas who subtly belittle us and intimidate us into thinking we have no place in how our political and cultural story is told. Cultivating our political literacy needn't be difficult, and we all engage politically, whether it's being invested in political conversations or actively supporting a campaign or policy or even buying products and choosing one over another. We don't know everything, but we can and should share the well-founded knowledge that we glean from our education and experiences.

If we doubt our agency, we might as well just purchase the prepared fruit bowls and premade vegetable dishes instead of making the effort to cook for ourselves. Prepackaged food that we don't have to spend time preparing might appeal to our senses of taste and laziness, but every time we break down the cost, we are reminded how we can make the same thing at home for much less and that it will be healthier and more filling. Until we take a chance and make our *own* smoothies in our *own* kitchens, we'll never realize how much tastier, cheaper, and healthier smoothies can be for us. By telling others how delicious it was to make something at home instead of always buying the prepared and premade option, we can influence entire budgets, meals, and taste buds. A little information and communication go a long way, especially if we trust what we know and are open to the things we don't.

X
Making Voices Heard through the Art of Storytelling

The worst illiterate is the political illiterate,
he doesn't hear, doesn't speak, nor participates
in the political events. He doesn't know the cost of life,
the price of the bean, of the fish, of the flour, of the rent,
of the shoes and of the medicine, all depends on political
decisions. The political illiterate is so stupid that he is proud
and swells his chest saying that he hates politics. The imbecile
doesn't know that, from his political ignorance is born
the prostitute, the abandoned child, and the worst thieves
of all, the bad politician, corrupted and flunky
of the national and multinational companies.

—Bertolt Brecht

We have mulled over how we can better feel, hear, navigate, articulate, identify truth from fraud, invite our friends into our vulnerable mental recesses, make honest arguments, survive piracy, and know better, and we'd like to finish this journey with you by mulling over the value of storytelling as we become more mindful shoppers and more politically literate citizens.

When done well, storytelling can do wonders. Successful merchants have figured out what their purposes and values are, and nothing conveys these as well as a story that captures people's attention. Some merchants tell a story where they are champions for consumer savings, yet others tell of their efforts to stand for uncompromising quality. Storytelling connects us, helps us make sense of the strange, and passes along our ethics and beliefs. A good story speaks to us in ways that numbers and data simply can't. The most effective stories dance with people's emotions and connect with people perhaps even more deeply than experts realize. We humans remember stories far better than we remember facts because our brains don't effectively distinguish between something we hear or read about and something that actually happened to us.

Remember dopamine? The brain releases copious amounts of the chemical when we experience emotionally charged events. In this way, dopamine allows us to more reliably process, retain, and recall a good story. Successful merchants and retailers make use of the dopamine effect and are not afraid to tell stories about their struggles, conflicts, setbacks, successes, and risks in bringing you their wares. Effective storytelling is rewarded by long-term brand loyalty that taps into the inherent human yearning for connection and informs their marketing strategies.

As consumers, we, too, get to tell a story. We tend to envision that we weave our shopping habits and purchasing decisions into the individual stories we tell throughout or lives. How we buy our everyday necessities, how often we decide to treat ourselves, and where we choose to get gifts for others tells a continuing story about our values. Where and how we invest time and money is one of the most powerful ways for us to show how we support global and local communities. One story we tell by our consuming choices might include how we choose to not buy what we don't need, thereby painting an image of responsible living and reliable decision-making. Those of us who want to write a story of compassion might elect to shop from local merchants instead of making distant conglomerates wealthier. The ethical impact of how we acquire our merchandise might write a story about boycotting and informing others about how big box stores don't agree with our moral standards. Money that we don't spend at places we feel are heartless institutions can be used at places that help communities that are less fortunate and take action against social injustices in whatever way they are able.

In the marketplace the consumer writes the story. Businesses that want to make a profit and grow must ultimately respond to consumer needs and demands. Each purchase is a vote. Every time we buy at a local business, our story conveys that our community is more important to us than a multinational behemoth. If we buy fresh produce instead of processed food, we tell the world how much we want healthy and safe food. When we buy from a business owned by women or people of color, our story speaks of our support of an inclusive economy. Even when we don't buy something, we tell the world that we are the kind of people who understand we don't always need stuff to live our best life. In this way, shopping is a political act.

History has illustrated time and time again how easy it is for politicians to say one thing while running for office and then do the opposite once they are elected. After a while a percentage of the citizenry eventually grows disenchanted with the politicians who betray their principles and abandon the will of those who trusted them with power. The market works much differently; in retail, consumers reign supreme and ultimately make all the decisions. When we vote in the marketplace with our time and money and by word of mouth, we get to determine which products, businesses, and industries survive and which ones fail. With this power we consumers create more economic wealth and jobs than any politician.

While boycotts have had varying success throughout history, they have given us the power to hold the attention of companies we engage with and intimidate those with whom we disagree. While boycotts are often politically motivated, we can simply choose not to offer our business to a certain store or company by how we judge the nobility and sustainability of its policies and practices. If we become unsatisfied with the product return policy of a store, how a store treats their customers or their staff, or where the store sources its products from, we take our business elsewhere. Our action sends the signal that we're not a happy consumer, we will not be a repeat customer, and we'll likely dissuade others from shopping there. This individual decision has far-reaching implications as businesses of every kind depend on consumer spending to exist. As a conscientious consumer, you can wield this power effectively against unethical corporate behaviors, and by word of mouth, you can educate others to do the same.

Every. Single. Consumer. Matters.

If we consumers do not want to purchase a product, we aren't obligated to. But if we disagree with a politician who is elected to office and that politician passes laws we disagree with, we must follow such laws, or we face certain consequences. In most of the world's economies, our purchasing power and our decisions offer us an opportunity to voice our opinions. Deciding how to spend money speaks as loudly as voting in an election. It benefits all if we all see that this is the story that we citizens are writing all our lives.

Shopkeepers, news broadcasters, and politicians all either pretend or assume that we know nearly as much about their items and policies as they do. Then again, we can't help but think that these voices of control and authority are even more oblivious about the environments in which they operate than we are. Sometimes politicians and retailers employ terms that need to be explained to the general public, but nobody does the explaining. Everyone either assumes they know what is being discussed or takes advantage of the ignorance while suggesting that everyone knows what's what.

Providing context in merchandise descriptions can help customers out. Merchants can adapt their sales language to be more widely understood. Product descriptions and technical terms could be used more honestly with just a bit of authentic clarification. That way, people would be more aware of what they were getting into with each purchase, thereby exercising greater agency in their own story.

In both retail and in politics, people talk about such abstract values as truth, loyalty, and commitment. When values are referred to so vaguely, they risk becoming abstract notions that mean different things to different people or carry little worthwhile meaning at all. It benefits shoppers and citizenry alike when everyone speaks the language that is used both in sales and political theater.

Terms that are used often and mean something different to different minds include:

> **Capital:** Money and wealth. The means to acquire goods and services, especially in a nonbarter system. Goods available for use as a factor of production, such as equipment and structures.
> **Civic:** Relating to cities and towns or the duties and activities of the people in them.
> **Corporation:** A group of individuals created by law, having a continuous existence independent of the existences of its members, and powers and liabilities distinct from those of its members.
> **Economy:** Collective focus of the study of money, currency and trade, and the efficient use of resources. The holistic system of production and distribution and consumption. The measure of a currency system; as the national economy.
> **Media:** How information is delivered and shared within a society.

Network: A group of interconnected people, systems, or things.
Partisan: Support of a particular cause or political party.
Peer: Someone who is an equal, based on age, education, status, training, or some other characteristic.
Political science: A social science that deals with the governing of people, largely by elected officials and governments.
Poll: To sample the opinions of people and tally the total with a survey or vote.
Resource: Something that one uses to achieve objective (e.g., raw materials or personnel).
Right: A legal or moral entitlement.
Security: The condition of not being threatened, especially physically, psychologically, emotionally, or financially. Proof of ownership of investment instruments.
Services: That which is produced, then traded, bought or sold, then finally consumed and consists of an action or work.
Zero-sum thinking, or **zero-sum bias:** a cognitive bias used to describe when a person believes that a situation is a matter of win-lose or loss-gain. In other words, they believe one person's loss is another person's gain.

Something that might be overlooked is the value in looking closely at our own stories to better understand our purposes and motivations. What guides us to make the decisions that we make, what keeps us committed to our chosen paths, and what is it that pushes us to change our behaviors? To understand why we chose what we did is to know what stories we write. It is that knowledge that allows people to best attain a sense of agency. Agency is what empowers us and gives us authorship over our own stories rather than be manipulated so thoroughly by others or our environment. Agency is one of the privileges and responsibilities of being human, and it helps to avert imposter syndrome. When we human beings can identify and narrate the experiences that inform our motivations, we are inspired with an unstoppable purpose, and we connect with others on a more human level than ever.

Writing the story of our own lives and connecting with others helps us to navigate through life with agency, but writing the story of all of us is something few manage to do but many compete for. The stories we tell are reflected in the systems that organize our societies. In some cultures, voters elect the country's head of state or president to officially represent them. Sometimes a legislative body is elected by the people and, in turn, chooses the head of the government or a dedicated group to implement laws and run the government on a day-to-day basis. Such organizational models tell a story about how cultures view collective trust, individual power, and how best to work in social groups to work toward shared goals.

As we learn more about ourselves, each other, and our environment, we adapt via system reform much the same way that we hear about better products at a new market and adapt our personal schedule accordingly. Reformers strive to improve governments as they regularly reflect on how well their systems are working and make the argument for improvements and policy changes. Such is the story of human progress. Writing it requires skill and luck, but human progress is more tenacious than perhaps most casual observers realize—if they only pay attention to conventional news.

By acting with agency, ordinary people like us can articulate our passions and values more effectively, especially if we make the effort to become a more politically literate culture, no matter the culture we identify with. Worldwide there is evidence that political literacy broadens individual and collective political knowledge and presents a clear advantage for populations. A misinformed public and a manipulated heart can hardly be expected to make wise decisions, so increasing political awareness in this way allows citizens to effect positive change in their culture. If citizens reflect critically upon the problems they see around them, such as power manipulation, lawful cruelty, or oppression of the weak, such honest, thoughtful reflection will tell a story that champions the values of the many. Such a politically literate culture is characterized as willing to test new ideas. This enlightened population realizes that life, and the world, is complex and is constantly changing. Becoming aware of the fallacies and tricks that the powers play on us allows us to sidestep obvious, easy, or preferred conclusions. Thinking critically and reanalyzing what our senses are telling us doesn't come easy to us, but that's what allows us to become wiser and more open-minded beings who understand that we can make a difference.

Politically literate people know that participation is key. It is vital to understand that everyone has their own opinions and that our peers, family members, leaders, and even children might not think about official policies the way we'd prefer they did. Agreeing about our politics should not be our main concern, but discussing ideas and helping each other tell our story are. While there might be a feeling that we lack sufficient knowledge about how government works or what the mediascape is telling us, by now we hope that you feel better equipped and prepared to take over more of our cultural story rather than succumb to the intimidation most of us are encouraged to feel.

While most people do not think they are powerful enough to effect change, noble change has always come from ordinary people. The powers aren't interested in changing society for the better. Why would they? The conditions that we see as ripe for improvement are the same conditions that give the privilege. The authority to put our values into action is within all of us as humans. There is something magical about the moment when we discover our own agency, but it is almost divine when we get to tell a story that depicts the essence of our work, our passions, our values, and our lives.

That spark of recognition when you see a familiar face across a crowded room makes you realize that our shared story allows us to overcome our flaws, biases, and setbacks to build a trust, a friendship, a respect, a culture. We hope that this journey you have taken with us has told a story about how political literacy is not only healthy and encouraged but also essential for future cultures to continue the story. With heart and mind, anyone can add to the great narrative with their own unique choices, whether it's campaigning for office, arguing for a more compassionate policy, or having meaningful conversations about the issues that matter most to you.

Keeping everything in mind that has been discussed, you can see how important it is for us to make our voices heard. Just because we know that the next supermarket we will visit has effective mechanisms in place designed to make us spend more money doesn't mean we should stop shopping altogether. It means we should be more mindful about ourselves and the environment that is acting upon us. That way we can make the best decisions we are equipped to make in any given circumstance and be proud of how we have acted. Remember, there is always more for us to learn about how we think and what others know about us.

Shop around.
Shop smart.
Be heard.

RELEVANT READING
AND ALL-ROUND USEFUL INFORMATION

Amnå, E., & Ekman, J. (2014). Standby citizens: Diverse faces of political passivity. *European Political Science Review 6*, 261–281. http://dx.doi.org/10.1017/S175577391300009X.

Amnå, E., Ekström, M., Kerr, M., & Stattin, H. (2009). Political socialization and human agency: The development of civic engagement from adolescence to young adulthood. *Statsvetenskaplig tidskrift 111*(1), 27–40.

Angvik, M., von Borries, B. (1997) *A Comparative European Survey on Historical Consciousness and Political Attitudes among Adolescents*. Korber-Stiftung.

Atkinson, L. (2012). Buying in to social change: How private consumption choices engender concern for the collective. *The ANNALS of the American Academy of Political and Social Science 644*(1), 191–206. http://dx.doi.org/10.1177/0002716212448366.

Bennett, W. L., Wells, C., & Freelon, D. (2011). Communicating civic engagement: Contrasting models of citizenship in the youth web sphere. *Journal of*

Communication 61, 835-856. http://dx.doi.org/10.1111/j.1460-2466.2011.01588.x.

Biesta, G., Lawy, R., & Kelly, N. (2009). Understanding young people's citizenship learning in everyday life. The role of contexts, relationships and dispositions. *Education, Citizenship and Social Justice 4*, 5-24. http://dx.doi.org/10.1177/1746197908099374

Dalton, R. J. (2008). Citizenship norms and the expansion of political participation. *Political Studies 56*, 76-98.

Furlong, A., & Cartmel, F. (2007). *Young People and Social Change*. Open University Press.

Haines, N. (1967) *Person to Person*. Macmillan.

Harris, A., Wyn, J., & Younes, S. (2010). Beyond apathetic or activist youth: "Ordinary" young people and contemporary forms of participation. *Young 18*, 9-32. http://dx.doi.org/10.1177/110330880901800103

Heater, D. (1969). *The Teaching of Politics*. Methuen.

Jones, J. P. (2006). A cultural approach to the study of mediated citizenship. *Social Semiotics 16*, 365-383. http://dx.doi.org/10.1080/10350330600664912

Kahneman, D. (2003). Maps of bounded rationality: psychology for behavioral economics. *American Economic Review 9* (5), 449-475.

Kershaw, I. (1981) A Critical View of the Conference. In Morrissett, I., Williams, A. (1981) *Social/Political Education in Three Countries*. SSEC.

Mercer, G. (1973) Political Education and Socialisation to Democratic Norms. University of Strathclyde.

Norris, P. (2004, November). Young people & political activism: From the politics of loyalties to the politics of choice? Report for the Council of Europe Symposium: "Young people and democratic institutions: from disillusionment to participation." Strasbourg.

Putnam, R. D. (2000). *Bowling Alone*. Simon & Schuster.

Rheingold, H. (2008). Using participatory media and public voice to encourage civic engagement. In W. L. Bennett (Ed.), Civic life online. Learning how digital media can engage youth (pp. 97–118). MIT Press.

Ridley, F. (1985) What Adults? What Politics? In *Political Education for Adults*.

Ross, A. (1987) Political Education in the Primary School. In Harber, C. (Ed.) (1987) *Political Education in Britain*. Falmer Press.

Scruton, R., Ellis-Jones, A., O'Keefe, D. (1985) *Education and Indoctrination*. Education Research Centre.

Shah, D. V., McLeod, D. M., Kim, E., Lee, S. Y., Gotlieb, M. R., Ho, S. S., & Brevik, H. (2007). Political consumerism: How communication and consumption orientations drive "lifestyle politics." *Annals of the American Academy of Political and Social Science 611*, 217–235. http://dx.doi.org/10.1177/0002716206298714.

Shehata, A., Ekström, M., & Olsson, T. (2014, May). Developing self-actualizing and dutiful citizens: Testing the AC-DC model using panel data among adolescents. Paper presented at the 64th Annual Conference of the International Communication Association, Seattle.

Smith, N., Lister, R., Middleton, S., & Cox, L. (2005). Young people as real citizens: Towards an inclusionary understanding of citizenship. *Journal of Youth Studies 8*, 425–443.

Sveningsson, M. (2013). "We're not like politically active or so, but we do have opinions." Young people's representations of political participation and citizenship. Paper presented at the 12th Nordic Youth Research Symposium (NYRIS) "Changing Societies and Cultures: Youth in the Digital Age," Tallinn, Estonia.

Wells, C. (2014). Two eras of civic information and the evolving relationship between civil society organizations and young citizens. *New Media & Society 16*, 615–636. http://dx.doi.org/10.1177/1461444813487962.

Printed in the USA
CPSIA information can be obtained
at www.ICGtesting.com
LVHW011945200324
774978LV00002B/38